CfE Higher
ENGLISH
SUCCESS GUIDE

PROSE

ANALYSIS

Poetry

Setting

COUPLET

DRAMA

Evaluation

Stagecraft

UNDERSTANDING

Plot

Rhyme

CfE Higher ENGLISH SUCCESS GUIDE

Iain Valentine

Contents

Contents

Who needs this book?

If you are studying Higher English this year you will already be aware of the challenges that face you: you might know someone who has sat previous versions of this exam; you might have looked at an SQA past paper; your teacher might have talked about the 'big jump' required from National 5 English. Whatever your thoughts and feelings about Higher English, there is no doubt that it can appear a rather daunting prospect and one that a good number of candidates find difficult each year.

Higher English can sometimes appear daunting simply because of the importance placed on this qualification. Even with all the changes to SQA exams in recent years, the status of Higher English remains unchanged. You might require a pass in this subject in order to gain entry to the university or college course that you have always wanted to do. Potential employers will often require job applicants to have a pass in Higher English because it shows you are an effective thinker and communicator – someone who can read and write and talk and listen at a detailed and complex level. To put it simply, our society *values* Higher English. Higher English requires hard work from you but obtaining this qualification will give *you* more choices in life.

But you should also *enjoy* the experience of studying for this qualification. Whatever literature you study and whatever language activities you undertake as part of your course you should come out at the end with a real sense that you have experienced something worthwhile – something that has made you look at yourself, other people and the world in a different way.

This book is designed to help you cope with the challenges you will face as you work your way towards the final examination. It is designed to maximise your chances of success. Think of it as your own secret weapon in your battle against the mighty Scottish Qualifications Authority (SQA). Who needs this book? You do.

Course structure and assessment

First of all the good news. If you have already studied English at National 5 level you will recognise most of the elements of your new Higher course.

The units

The Higher English course consists of two units:

1. Creation and Production (Writing and Talking)
2. Analysis and Evaluation (Reading and Listening).

The assessments

To pass these units you must successfully complete the following internal assessments (marked by your teacher/assessor):

• Unit assessment – evidence of Writing (Creation and Production)	
• Unit assessment – evidence of Talking (Creation and Production)	
• Unit assessment – evidence of Reading (Analysis and Evaluation)	
• Unit assessment – evidence of Listening (Analysis and Evaluation).	

There is more information on unit assessment on pages 12–21.

In order to pass Higher English (the SQA calls it 'gaining a course award'), you will have to pass the **internal assessment** (the units mentioned above) and the **external assessment** (the exam and the Portfolio of Writing). The internal assessment is marked by your teachers and the external assessment is marked by the SQA.

The external assessment

The following external assessment will be marked by the SQA:

- A Portfolio of Writing worth **30 marks**. You have to send **two** pieces of writing to the SQA. One must be **creative**. The SQA guidelines specify the following possibilities for your creative piece:
  - ➤ a personal reflective essay
  - ➤ a piece of prose fiction (e.g. short story, episode from a novel)

➢ a poem or set of thematically linked poems

➢ a dramatic script (e.g. scene, monologue, sketch).

One piece of writing must be **discursive**. The SQA guidelines specify the following possibilities for this piece:

- a persuasive essay

- an argumentative essay

- a report

- a piece of transactional writing.

You will be given opportunities to plan, draft and redraft these pieces but they must be all your own work. You can even write one or both pieces in Scots if you want. Each folio piece is marked out of **15**. It is vital that you work hard on your portfolio because it is the one piece of external assessment that is totally under your control.

Further external assessment by the SQA is as follows:

- Exam Question Paper 1 – Reading for Understanding, Analysis and Evaluation (**1 hour and 30 minutes**), worth **30 marks**. In this paper you have to answer questions on two non-fiction passages.

- Exam Question Paper 2 – Critical Reading (**1 hour and 30 minutes**). This consists of:

    ➢ Section 1 – questions on Scottish texts (one context question), worth **20 marks**. In this part of the paper you will answer questions on a Scottish text or an extract from a Scottish text you have already studied.

    ➢ Section 2 – one critical essay, worth **20 marks**. In this part of the paper you will be given a choice of essay topics. You will write about a text (or texts) you have studied during your course. You can choose from Drama, Prose (fiction or non-fiction), Poetry, Film and Television Drama. You can even write about a Language topic if you wish.

In your course you will probably study three different genres of texts including one or perhaps two of the specified Scottish texts.

The SQA has specified the following Scottish texts for study from 2014 onwards but you should note that this list might change every few years or so.

Drama

The Cheviot, The Stag and The Black, Black Oil by John McGrath

Men Should Weep by Ena Lamont Stewart

The Slab Boys by John Byrne

Prose

Short stories by Iain Crichton Smith. *The Red Door, The Telegram, Mother and Son, In Church, The Painter, The Crater*

The Cone-Gatherers by Robin Jenkins

Short stories by George Mackay Brown. *A Time to Keep, The Bright Spade, The Wireless Set, The Whaler's Return, The Eye of the Hurricane, Tartan*

Sunset Song by Lewis Grassic Gibbon

The Trick is to Keep Breathing by Janice Galloway

Poetry

Carol Ann Duffy

War Photographer, Havisham, Valentine, Originally, Anne Hathaway, Mrs Midas

Norman MacCaig

Sounds of the Day, Assisi, Visiting Hour, Memorial, Aunt Julia, Basking Shark

Sorley MacLean

Hallaig, Screapadal, Heroes, Shores, An Autumn Day, I Gave You Immortality

Don Paterson

Waking with Russell, The Thread, 11:00: Baldovan, Two Trees, The Ferryman's Arms, Nil Nil

Liz Lochhead

The Bargain, My Rival's House, View of Scotland/Love Poem,

Some Old Photographs, For my Grandmother Knitting, Last Supper

Robert Burns

Holy Willie's Prayer, Tam O'Shanter, To a Mouse, A Poet's Welcome to his Love-Begotten Daughter, Address to the Deil, A Man's a Man for a' That

You will use your knowledge of these texts to answer the question on Scottish texts **and** (if you study more than one set text) to write a critical essay.

The marks for your external assessment will be added up and converted into a grade from A–D.

In order to give yourself the best possible chance to succeed in this subject, you *must* be prepared to spend a significant amount of your own time studying and revising.

It is a good idea to keep a record of your assessments as you work your way through the course. Your teacher or tutor will probably provide you with one or you can use something like the record shown on the following page.

Higher English student record

Unit	Outcome	Date: Pass/fail:	Reassessment date: Pass/fail:
Creation and production	*Writing* • at least one written text using detailed and complex written language		
	Talking • at least one spoken interaction using detailed and complex language		
Analysis and evaluation	*Reading* • understanding, analysing and evaluating at least one detailed and complex written text		
	Listening • understanding, analysing and evaluating at least one detailed and complex spoken language activity		

Writing portfolio

Creative	Title	Estimated mark/15	Selected for folio?
a personal essay/ reflective essay			
a piece of prose fiction (e.g. short story, episode from a novel)			
a poem or set of thematically linked poems			
a dramatic script (e.g. scene, monologue, sketch)			

Writing portfolio

Discursive	Title	Estimated mark/15	Selected for folio?
a persuasive essay			
an argumentative essay			
a report for a specified purpose			
a piece of transactional writing			
		Total folio estimate	/30

Prelim examination

	Marks	Comments
Reading	/30	
Scottish text question	/20	
Critical essay	/20	
	Total /70	

Final estimate > SQA	Overall percentage	Grade/band
Prelim + Writing Portfolio (70% + 30%)		

Genres of literature

You should study at least three **different** genres of literature as part of your course and as preparation for the final exam.

The only compulsory requirement is the need to study at least **one** of the specified Scottish texts so there is a wide variety of possible combinations of texts to study.

For example, the literature element of your course might involve you studying:

- Poetry – the six specified poems by Don Paterson
- Prose – *The Cone-Gatherers*
- Drama – *Othello*

OR

- Poetry – the six specified poems by Carol Ann Duffy
- Prose – *One Flew over the Cuckoo's Nest*
- Drama – *A View from the Bridge*

OR

- Poetry – a selection of poems by contemporary writers
- Prose – *Sunset Song*
- Film and TV drama – *Goodfellas*

OR

- Poetry – the six specified poems by Robert Burns
- Prose – the six specified stories by George Mackay Brown
- Drama – *Men Should Weep*

OR

- Poetry – a selection of Philip Larkin's poems
- Prose – *The Trick is to Keep Breathing*
- Drama – *The Slab Boys*

OR

- Poetry – the six specified poems by Norman MacCaig
- Prose – a selection of non-fiction texts
- Drama – *Macbeth*

Some texts are common to National 5 and Higher (the MacCaig poetry and *The Cone-Gatherers* are two examples of this). If you studied any of these texts for National 5, don't overlook them as possible choices in the question on Scottish texts.

TOP TIP

Make sure that you study a wide range of literature/media during your course – you will get far more out of the course if you do so. It will also mean that you are more likely to encounter texts which interest you and candidates nearly always answer more effectively on texts they have enjoyed.

One other thing to bear in mind is that you are allowed to write a critical essay on **any text** as long as it is on a **different genre** from the text you chose in the Questions on Scottish Texts section of the paper. This means that you could, for example, write a critical essay on the Norman MacCaig poem printed in the question on Scottish texts, providing that you didn't answer on poetry in that section.

Let's say 'Sounds of the Day' was the MacCaig poem printed in the Scottish Texts section and the following question appeared in the Critical Essay section:

> *Choose a poem which features a relationship.*
>
> *Discuss how the poet's presentation of this relationship adds to your understanding of the central concerns of the poem.*
>
> SQA, Specimen Paper, Higher English 2014

You could then use 'Sounds of the Day' as the subject of your essay. This would have the obvious advantage of not requiring you to agonise over whether you have remembered lines of the poem to use to support your line of argument in the essay – it's all there in front of you!

Achieving success in the Creation and Production unit

Remember what we said about unit assessment in the chapter on the structure of your Higher course. Again much of this will be familiar to you if you have already completed a National 5 English course. There are two outcomes for the creation and production unit: **Writing** and **Talking**.

Writing

In order to pass the **Writing** outcome you must show that you can '**create and produce detailed and complex written texts**'. You will have to show that you can:

1.1   Select significant ideas and content, using a format and structure appropriate to purpose and audience

1.2   Apply knowledge and understanding of language in terms of language choice and technical accuracy

1.3   Communicate meaning at a first reading

To achieve the outcome you only have to demonstrate these skills in **one** piece of writing.

The piece of writing used as assessment evidence for this unit might come from a unit of work that forms part of your course or it might be a 'stand alone' activity given by your teacher. The piece of writing used as assessment evidence for the Creation and Production unit can also be submitted to the SQA as part of your Writing Portfolio.

The production of your piece of writing should involve the following stages:

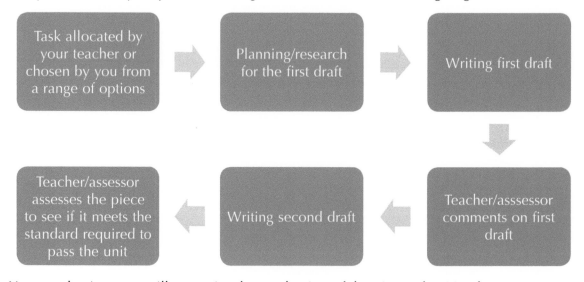

Task allocated by your teacher or chosen by you from a range of options → Planning/research for the first draft → Writing first draft → Teacher/asssessor comments on first draft → Writing second draft → Teacher/assessor assesses the piece to see if it meets the standard required to pass the unit

Your teacher/assessor will supervise the production of the piece of writing but you are allowed to complete the work outside of the classroom. You will not be allowed to redraft the piece of writing more than once. The writing must be all your own work so you must be very careful to avoid any sort of plagiarism. Always ask your teacher/assessor if you have any questions about this.

What to include in different types of writing

If the task requires you to produce a piece of **discursive writing** it should incorporate the following features:

- appropriate content
- appropriate structure
- evidence of research
- a clear line of thought (or argument)
- skilful use of linking words
- the use of evidence to support the points you make
- the use of rhetorical devices (if the purpose of the piece is to persuade the reader) – rhetorical question, hyperbole, convincing use of statistics etc.
- appropriate sentence structures
- consistently accurate paragraphing, punctuation and spelling.

If the task requires you to produce a piece of **reflective writing** it should incorporate the following features:

- genuine engagement with the topic
- appropriate structure
- evidence of your personality
- insight into the topic
- reflective language, which reveals what you think about the topic
- effective use of word choice, imagery and sentence structure
- consistently accurate paragraphing, punctuation and sentence construction.

If the task requires you to produce a piece of **prose fiction** (such as a short story) it should incorporate the following features:

- appropriate structure (don't forget to think about the ending)
- techniques appropriate to the short story genre
- development of setting and characterisation
- evidence of insight and developed thought
- effective use of word choice, imagery and sentence structure
- consistently accurate paragraphing, punctuation and spelling.

There is more detailed advice on how to produce different kinds of writing in the writing portfolio chapter on pages 100–117.

Talking

In order to pass the **Talking** outcome you have to '**Participate in detailed and complex spoken activities**'. In fact what you have to do is very similar to what you have to do to achieve the Writing outcome. You will have to show that you can:

2.1   Select significant ideas and content, using a format and structure appropriate to purpose and audience

2.2   Apply knowledge and understanding of language in terms of language choice

2.3   Communicate meaning at first hearing

2.4   Use significant aspects of non-verbal communication

The 'spoken activities' might involve you talking about something you are working on as part of the course such as one of the poems or short stories you are studying; it might be linked to a writing activity or it might be another 'stand alone' task. You can achieve the outcome either by delivering an individual presentation to an audience or taking part in a group discussion.

Individual presentation

A successful individual presentation will include most of the following features:

- an effective line of argument or thought
- not being over-reliant on notes
- detailed and complex ideas
- effective use of linking words
- an appropriate structure
- points that are developed in detail
- effective use of evidence to back up the points being made
- rhetorical devices (rhetorical question, repetition, hyperbole etc.)
- appropriate tone and register
- appropriate sentence structures and vocabulary
- an appropriate speed of delivery
- some variety in the speaker's tone of voice
- few stumbles or hesitations
- consistent eye-contact with the audience
- use of gesture etc. if and when appropriate
- effective use of audio-visual materials to enhance the delivery of the talk.

Group discussion

A successful participant in group discussion will:

- contribute a good number of detailed ideas and opinions
- support/challenge/use/develop/summarise what other members of the group say
- support points made with detailed evidence
- use an appropriate tone and register (remember that you are being formally assessed)
- use language that is suitable for the topic being discussed (if you're discussing a literary text, you'll need to make use of appropriate literary terms)
- use appropriate sentence structures and vocabulary
- speak with few hesitations
- vary his or her tone of voice to add impact to what is said
- speak clearly and audibly
- maintain eye-contact with other members of the group
- use other non-verbal techniques such as gesture and facial expression.

TOP TIP

Remember that you must make a good number of contributions to the discussion but that you must **not** dominate it. It is every member of the group's responsibility to ensure that everyone gets involved.

Achieving success in the Analysis and Evaluation unit

Remember what we said about unit assessment in the chapter on the structure of your Higher course. Again much of this will be familiar to you if you have already completed a National 5 English course. There are two outcomes for the analysis and evaluation unit: **Reading** and **Listening**.

Reading 📖

In order to pass the **Reading** outcome you must show that you can '**understand, analyse and evaluate detailed and complex written texts**'. You will have to show that you can say what the intended audience for a piece of writing might be; what the main purpose is and what the main ideas are in the text. You will also demonstrate your knowledge and understanding of how a writer uses language to achieve meaning and to achieve particular effects. You must also demonstrate that you can use appropriate critical terms in your analysis. To achieve the outcome you only have to demonstrate these skills once.

There are several ways in which your teacher might assess you for this outcome. Your assessment might take the form of

- questions on a poem
- questions on an extract from a novel or a short story
- questions on a newspaper article (print or digital)
- questions on an extract from a drama text.

In fact the assessment might be on anything as long as the chosen text is 'detailed and complex' *and is something you haven't seen before.*

You might find that your teacher uses an extract from one of the Scottish texts you are studying this year as the basis of the assessment. Again, this is fine as long as you *have not yet been taught that particular poem or short story or that particular part of a novel or play.*

 Your answers to the questions might have to be written down or you might give them orally. If this is done orally, your teacher will keep a detailed checklist of your responses.

Reading outcomes

Let's look at what your unit assessment for Reading might look like. Here's a reminder of the outcomes:

1   Understand, analyse and evaluate detailed and complex written texts by:

1.1   Identifying and explaining the purpose and audience, as appropriate to genre

1.2   Identifying and explaining the main ideas and supporting details

1.3   Applying knowledge and understanding of language to explain meaning and effect in depth and detail, using appropriate critical terminology

Now read the following passage and have a go at answering the questions. (Answers on pages 118–120.)

TOP TIP

Use the same techniques to answer these questions as you do for the Reading for Understanding, Analysis and Evaluation paper in the exam.

The following article was written by Stuart Tootal, who served as a soldier in Afghanistan.

Post-traumatic stress disorder is the invisible scar of war

Not all Afghan veterans will suffer from mental trauma – but we owe a debt to those who do

1. As a soldier, I used to be sceptical about the significance of post-traumatic stress disorder (PTSD) – about the idea that strong men could be reduced to a shadow of their former selves by the experience of war. I might have stayed that way, had I not found myself commanding troops in Afghanistan.

2. In 2006, 3 Para was the first UK combat unit to be sent into Helmand province. Fifteen of my battle group were killed in action, and another 46 seriously wounded. By the time we returned to Britain, any cynicism had disappeared.

3. The fighting 3 Para engaged in has been described as the most intensive combat experienced by the British Army since the Korean War. Isolated bases came under constant attack from enemy assaults, mortars and rocket fire. Patrols were close-combat affairs in high-standing crops, where the Taliban could often be heard moving in the next stand of maize prior to the start of a firefight. The increasing sophistication of roadside bombs became an enduring dread.

4. While we, and the other Army and Marine units that followed us, served valiantly and admirably, the experience of Helmand left a mark on all of us: the loss of close friends and comrades, combat fatigue, the constant stress of facing death or serious injury. But while most of us readjusted to the peacetime world and reintegrated with our families, for some the mental trauma had become too deeply embedded.

5. Since 2006, hundreds of thousands of British troops have fought in Afghanistan. Numerous studies have indicated that between 10 and 20 per cent of soldiers returning from these combat zones are suffering, or will suffer, from PTSD. Yesterday, the charity Combat Stress announced that it has seen a 57 per cent increase in the number of Afghanistan-related referrals over the past year, from 228 to 358. Given the estimated incubation period of between seven to 14 years, there are bound to be many more.

6. But like shellshock during the First World War, and combat fatigue in the Second, PTSD remains a contentious issue. Official MoD (Ministry of Defence) figures claim that only 4 per cent of soldiers will suffer from it, although they accept that the level will be slightly higher for infantry units and among reservists (at 5 and 6 per cent respectively). But this calculation is based on a study completed in 2009. Since then, the UK has been at war for another five years, and thousands more have served. Additionally, the study did not track veterans, so cannot take account of the delayed onset of PTSD – which can often manifest itself when veterans leave the familiar environment of the military and enter civilian life.

7. This is not to suggest that the MoD has not acted. Post-tour decompression; education and training to identify and manage PTSD; 24-hour mental health lines; joint initiatives with the NHS – all have been put in place over the past few years. The Service charities have also worked hard to address the issue. However, there is still more that we can do, especially in regard to supporting those who leave the military. In 2012, 50 soldiers and veterans took their own lives – more than the number of combat casualties in the same year. And I continue to hear stories from former soldiers whose treatment for PTSD has fallen short of where it should be.

8. Given the number of British troops that have been exposed to the dehumanising effects of war in Afghanistan and the likely incubation periods associated with the condition, there is a compelling case to review the statistics and address the gaps in provision. But we also need to avoid exaggerating the extent of the mental trauma, and maligning those who suffer from it.

9. By no means will everyone who has served on combat operations succumb to PTSD – and even then, the condition does not prevent them from leading normal lives or holding down a meaningful job, with proper treatment and managerial support. My current employer, Barclays, has helped 2,350 veterans since 2010 via its Armed Forces Transition, Employment and Resettlement programme, and a small number have suffered from PTSD.

10. Our Servicemen and women are a remarkable fraternity, 'born from smoke, danger and death'. They know what real fear is and have to live with the consequences of the application and receipt of lethal force. Yet they are continuously prepared to risk life and limb in places such as Afghanistan to do the nation's bidding.

11. While not all will suffer from mental trauma, even the bravest of soldiers can succumb to the condition. We need to work together in the state, military and private sectors to understand and address PTSD as an invisible scar of war, and the natural – but treatable – consequence of combat.

Written by Stuart Tootal and published in
The Daily Telegraph on 13 May 2014.

Re-read paragraphs 1–3.

1. a) Summarise in your own words the change in Stuart Tootal's attitude to PTSD. (*Outcome 1.2*)

   b) Analyse how the writer's language in these paragraphs conveys the reality of combat. (*Outcome 1.3*)

Re-read paragraph 4.

2. Analyse how the writer uses sentence structure and word choice to highlight the soldiers' experiences in Afghanistan and their experiences in the 'peacetime world'. (*Outcome 1.3*)

Re-read paragraphs 6–8.

3. What do you think might be a reason for the level of PTSD being 'slightly higher for infantry units and reservists'? (*Outcome 1.2*)

4. Identify and explain the writer's use of irony in paragraph 7. (*Outcome 1.3*)

5. Explain in your own words the **four** main points the writer makes in paragraph 8. (*Outcome 1.2*)

Re-read paragraph 11.

6. The writer describes PTSD as 'an invisible scar of war'. Explain the meaning of this image and analyse its effect. (*Outcome 1.3*)

Consider the text as a whole.

7. What evidence is there in the passage of the support offered to serving soldiers and veterans? Answer in your own words. (*Outcome 1.2*)

8. Identify a purpose of this text. Explain your answer with close reference to the text. (*Outcome 1.1*)

9. A text may have many audiences. Identify a possible audience for this text, and explain your answer with close reference to the text. (*Outcome 1.1*)

There are no 'marks' for these questions. Your answers simply provide the evidence that you have achieved the outcomes. Your assessor (usually your class teacher) will decide whether or not you have met the requirements necessary for 1.1, 1.2 and 1.3.

For example, you'll notice that there are four questions on *Outcome 1.3* in the above assessment. Your assessor might only be looking for you to get two of these correct. Always ask your assessor if you are unsure about how many questions you need to answer correctly.

Listening 🎧

In order to pass the **Listening** outcome you have to do exactly the same as for Reading except that for **Listening** you are dealing with *spoken* texts.

To meet this outcome you must:

Understand, analyse and evaluate detailed and complex spoken texts by:

2.1   Identifying and explaining the purpose and audience, as appropriate to genre

2.2   Identifying and explaining the main ideas and supporting details

2.3   Applying knowledge and understanding of language to explain meaning and effect in depth and detail, using appropriate critical terminology

You will usually be given the questions before you listen to the text so that should make note taking easier for you. You will usually be allowed to listen to the text as often as you need to.

> **TOP TIP**
>
> When analysing spoken language, word choice, tone, imagery, rhetorical devices, repetition, alliteration and onomatopoeia are among the sort of features to consider.

Practice listening assessment

Here is a practice listening assessment for you to try.

You will be asked to listen to an extract from Radio 4's *Today* programme, available at http://www.bbc.co.uk/archive/hamlet/8537.shtml

Taking part in the discussion are:

- Evan Davies (the interviewer)
- Michael Billington (*The Guardian's* theatre critic)
- Simon Russell Beale (an actor).

In the extract Evan Davis asks theatre critic Michael Billington about the Royal Shakespeare Company's new production of *Hamlet*, starring 'Doctor Who' actor David Tennant. Simon Russell Beale joins their discussion.

The extract lasts approximately five minutes. Your assessor would probably play the extract at least twice, but you could always ask to hear it again. You may take notes as you listen to help you.

Patrick Stewart and David Tennant star in the RSC's Hamlet *at the Courtyard Theatre, Stratford-upon-Avon. Photograph: Tristram Kenton (photo. The Guardian).*

Answer the questions that follow.

1. What is Michael Billington's opinion of David Tennant's performance as Hamlet (*Outcome 2.2*) and how is this opinion conveyed through his language (*Outcome 2.3*)?

2. What is another reason for the success of this production of *Hamlet*? (*Outcome 2.2*)

3. What is Michael Billington's opinion of what it means to play Dr Who, as opposed to Hamlet, (*Outcome 2.2*) and how is this conveyed through his language (*Outcome 2.3*)?

4. What does Simon Russell Beale mean when he says that Hamlet is 'quite hospitable as a part'? (*Outcome 2.2*)

5. How does Simon Russell Beale's language help to convey the idea of 'hundreds of different types of Hamlets'? (*Outcome 2.3*)

6. Analyse how Michael Billington's use of language helps to emphasise the fact that this production is about more than just David Tennant as Hamlet. (*Outcome 2.3*)

7. Analyse Simon Russell Beale's description of what it is like to have played Hamlet. (*Outcome 2.3*)

8. What conclusion is reached at the end of the discussion? (*Outcome 2.2*)

9. Identify the **purpose** of this extract and explain why you think this, based on what you have heard in the extract (*Outcome 2.1*).

10. Identify one possible **audience** for the extract and explain why you think this, based on what you have heard in the extract (*Outcome 2.1*).

Again, there are no 'marks' for these questions. Your answers simply provide the evidence that you have achieved the outcomes. Your assessor (usually your class teacher) will decide whether or not you have met the requirements necessary for 2.1, 2.2 and 2.3.

Check your answers on pages 121–122.

How to study prose fiction (novels and short stories)

When you read a novel or a short story as part of your Higher course you need to be able to do more than just offer an opinion on it ('I really liked that.'; 'That was the dullest book I've ever read.'). You have to be able to analyse the techniques used by the writer in constructing the text and be able to say how effective you find them.

Structure

In some ways you are already an expert in this area. You've been hearing and reading and watching stories all your life. You already know how stories 'work'. You expect stories to have a beginning, a middle and an end. A more sophisticated description of this structure is as follows:

Exposition. The situation that exists at the start of the story. The reader is introduced to the characters, the setting is described and we are given an idea of what is going on. This is sometimes described as the 'equilibrium'.

Complication. Something happens to disturb the 'equilibrium' described at the start of the story and creates a problem for the central character(s).

Development. The 'chain of events' that takes place as characters attempt to deal with the problem.

Climax. The most exciting part of the story. Events come to a head.

Resolution. The strands of the plot are all worked out and a 'new equilibrium' is established.

A good number of the stories you will study will follow this pattern or 'classic narrative structure'. However, you need to be aware that a writer will sometimes play about with this structure in order to achieve particular effects. The writer might begin *in medias res*, in the middle of things, at some point in the development. This adds impact to the start of the story and will sometimes make it more dramatic. The writer might then use flashback to give the reader details of the exposition. The writer might not use any exposition at all until the end, leaving the reader to try and work out what is happening and why as the story goes along. There might be no resolution and the reader is left to ponder what happens next. Some modern writers have abandoned traditional structure entirely and leave you as the reader to create one as best you can as you read the 'story'.

The narrator

Ask yourself who is telling the story. Is it told by a character in the story in the **first person (I, me, we, us)**? If so, how does this affect our experience of reading the story? This technique might make us sympathise with the character as they become our 'representative' in the story – especially if they tell us their thoughts and feelings. Beware the **unreliable narrator** – a narrator who might not be telling us the truth or who might not know the truth of what is going on.

Is the story told in the **third person**, i.e. by someone who is not 'in' the story? If so it might be an **omniscient narrator** who can tell us everything that is going on and what all the characters are thinking. It might be a **limited narrator** who only tells us about a few characters and their actions and tells us much less about other characters and actions. It might be a **demonstrative narrator** who only reports what characters *say* and *do* leaving the reader to work out the motives behind these actions.

Characterisation

It is very important to remember the simple truth that characters in novels and short stories are not real. It is not your job to treat them as if they are real people with all the hopes, fears, failings and neuroses that make up our personalities, even although the writer might present them to us in a very convincing way. What is important is for you to be able to analyse *how* the characters are created by the writer.

Characters can be created through what they say – the dialogue in the story – and what they do – their actions. Remember that nothing is in a story by accident. Everything means something. Look at this extract from the opening chapter of a novel by the Scottish writer Andrew Greig. Notice how economically Greig introduces the characters of Murray and Tricia to the reader through what they say and what they do. The extract is a good example of the **omniscient narrator** at work and you should notice how skilfully the writer suggests the characters' thoughts.

Even in Kirkintilloch the sun was shining as Murray Hamilton eased the screws off the front licence plate on his old Kawasaki. His-eleven-year old sat on the steps of the council house with her guitar, hesitating between one chord and the next. His boy Jamie was kicking a football against the lean-to.

'So,' Tricia said, 'is this the end of a glittering political career?'

He took the new plate from her and squinted into the light. Five years on the Council till he'd resigned, a thousand committee meetings, ten thousand doorsteps – and what had changed?

'Time to try anither way, Trish.'

The thread caught in the bolt and he began to tighten.

'You'll not be much of a dad in jail.'

He put down the spanner.

'I'll stop right now if you want me tae.'

Behind them Eve at last found the new chord and strummed it cautiously.

'I just said be careful. And don't get hurt.'

'Right darlin.'

Tricia began loosening the rear plate. She glanced at her husband's bowed head and for the first time saw that his tight red-gold hair was starting to thin around the crown, and the edge of his beard was touched with grey like the first touch of frost. Still, she grinned, as she put the screws down carefully beside her. Might as well be a bit daft before we're all past it.

Andrew Greig, *The Return of John MacNab*

When describing a character to the reader, sometimes the narrator will just tell the reader what a character is like:

John Rhodes, when he came, was big and fair ... The face was slightly pockmarked. The eyes were pleasantly blue.

William McIlvanney, *Laidlaw*

But often the narrator's word choice or use of imagery will have *connotations* that the reader is expected to pick up on. What does the simile in the next extract suggest about John Rhodes?

'Hullo, you,' he said to Laidlaw and sat down across the table from them. 'Ye'll hiv a drink.'

'A whisky for me,' Laidlaw said. 'With water.'

'I won't bother, thank you,' Harkness said.

The blue eyes turned on him like a blowtorch lit but not yet shooting flame.

William McIlvanney, *Laidlaw*

Sentence structure

Don't forget to look for the effects created by the writer using sentences of different lengths and types. For example, the use of very long sentences with lots of punctuation might suggest things happening quickly or all at once. A series of short sentences might suggest rising tension or fear.

Mood

You should think of the *mood* of a piece of writing as the feeling or emotion or *atmosphere* the writer is trying to create in a piece of writing. Is it happy, gloomy, bleak, sympathetic … ? This can be achieved by reference to things like the weather (just think about the different moods suggested by a storm on an isolated moor and a morning of bright sunshine on a holiday beach) or to different colours (black has connotations very different to that of white).

Look at this extract from the opening of another of Andrew Greig's novels. By closely examining word choice, imagery and sentence structure, see if you can spot *how* Greig creates a gloomy or downbeat mood.

A man on a motorbike finally came to the end of the road.

He sat astride contemplating gate, padlock, chain. Once he would have felt compelled to do something about those. Instead he switched off, unstrapped his helmet and let sound in.

Eight miles into the Rothiemurchus Forest, towards the end of a short winter's day, the world was quiet. No human voices, no birdsong, just a hiss of water from melting snow, damp wind seeping through the pines.

He got stiffly off the bike, clipped the helmet over the handlebars, climbed the gate and walked up the snowy path through the dark wood. He wore camouflage trousers and jacket but did not look like a soldier – at least, not from a war that anyone had won. After a hundred yards he paused, tossed the ignition key into the undergrowth and trudged on …

… He took a smaller path and then a smaller one off that. At a ghostly intersection he stood in the rapidly fading light, pulled off his gloves and hurled one after the other into the darkness under the trees.

A while later, he unstrapped his watch, dropped it without breaking stride. He had no further need of time.

The last days had been a matter of discarding, in order, the remaining things that mattered to him. There was little left now. The pack was empty so he hung it dark and drooping on a branch, like a crow left by gamekeepers.

Andrew Greig, *Romanno Bridge*

How to study poetry

When you are first faced with a poem you should approach the text by asking the following questions:

Understanding	What is the poem about?	Look at the content, mood, attitude of the poet, subject or aspect of life revealed in the poem.
Analysis	Who is speaking?	The poet? Or has a persona been adopted? How do you know?
Analysis	How is the poem structured?	Regular structure or not? Look at stanza form, line length, rhyme, rhythm.
Analysis	What other techniques have been used?	Look at word choice, imagery (simile, metaphor, personification), sentence structure, sound.
Evaluation	How effective are the poet's methods in conveying the meaning of the text to the reader?	Think about your reaction to the poem as a piece of literature.

Annotate your copy whenever possible. Mark it in any way that helps you to think about the text. There will be lines you find difficult to understand but don't forget that the poem is not a 'puzzle' with only one 'solution' or 'right answer'. Ambiguity is an important concept in poetry – any poem might have more than one 'meaning'.

Here's a reminder of some of the technical terms you need to know:

Alliteration	Words beginning with the same consonant sound. Creates a pattern of sounds for a particular effect.

	Wee, sleekit, cowrin', tim'rous beastie,
	 O, whit a panic's in thy breastie!
	 Thou need na start awa sae hasty,
	     Wi' bickering brattle!
	
	                 Robert Burns, 'To a Mouse'

Association	Poems usually *suggest* more to the reader than they state. Poets want you to make associations based on the words on the page. Allusions, references, analogies, images, metaphors, similes all help you to employ associations.
Caesura	A pause within a line of poetry. Such pauses can break up the rhythm or meter of a poem. A thing of beauty is a joy forever: Its loveliness increases; it will never Pass into nothingness; but still will keep A bower quiet for us, and a sleep Full of sweet dreams, and health, and quiet breathing. John Keats, 'Endymion'

Connotation	What the word *suggests* rather than what it simply *means* (denotation), e.g. 'sunset' means the time of day when the sun slips below the horizon (denotation), but 'sunset' might also suggest ending, something drawing to a close, or even something like death (connotation).
Dramatic monologue	A poem in which an imaginary speaker addresses an imaginary audience. In 'My Last Duchess' Robert Browning adopts the persona of the Duke of Ferrara negotiating terms prior to acquiring his latest wife. The poem reveals what happened to his previous wife!
	That's my last Duchess painted on the wall,
	Looking as if she were alive. I call
	That piece a wonder, now: Frà Pandolf's hands
	Worked busily a day and there she stands.
	Robert Browning, 'My Last Duchess'
Elegy	A serious and formal poem usually inspired by a person's death.
Ellipsis	Missing out words from a sentence.
End-stopped line	A line of poetry that ends in a pause of some kind – indicated by appropriate punctuation.
Enjambment	Where the meaning, punctuation, and sound of a poem do not stop at the end of a line but run on into the next. These two verses of a poem by Carol Ann Duffy show examples of both end-stopped lines and enjambment.
	I longed for Rome, home, someone else. When the Nazarene
	Entered Jerusalem, my maid and I crept out,
	Bored stiff, disguised, and joined the frenzied crowd,
	I tripped, clutched the bridle of an ass, looked up
	And there he was. His face? Ugly. Talented.
	He looked at me. I mean he looked at *me*. My God.
	His eyes were eyes to die for. Then he was gone,
	His rough men shouldering a pathway to the gates.
	Carol Ann Duffy, 'Pilate's Wife'
Free verse	Poetry that has no regular rhyme or rhythm. Theme, images and layout are likely to provide a poem written in free verse with form.

Imagery	Pictures in words. Poets use images to make us recreate imaginatively what is being described. See how economically Norman MacCaig does this in his poem, 'February – Not Everywhere'. Such days, when trees run downwind, their arms stretched before them. Such days, when the sun's in a drawer and the drawer locked. When the meadow is dead, is a carpet, thin and shabby, with no pattern and at bus stops people retract into collars their faces like fists. And when, in a firelit room, mother looks at her four seasons, at her little boy, in the centre of everything, with still pools of shadows and a fire throwing flowers.
Inversion	Changing around (inverting) the usual or expected sequence of words in a sentence. Inversion enables a poet to draw attention to a particular word or idea.
Lyric	A shorter poem, which expresses the poet's thoughts and feelings.
Metaphor	The simplest way to think of this is comparison where one thing is described as being something else. Look again at 'February – Not Everywhere' (above) for some good examples.
Metre	The regular pattern of stressed and unstressed syllables in a poem.
Parody	A poem that imitates another for comic effect.
Persona	An identity assumed by the poet. Remember that the 'I' in the poem may not actually be the poet, it could be an entirely imaginary person. I'm not the first or the last to stand on a hillock, watching the man she married prove to the world he's a total, utter, absolute, Grade A pillock. Carol Ann Duffy, 'Mrs Icarus'
Rhyme	Words that have identical sounds, usually at the ends of lines. The rhyme inevitably links the words rhymed and hence their meanings and associations. 'Half-rhyme' is a rhyme that *almost* rhymes.

Rhyme-scheme	The pattern of rhyme within a poem. Letters are used to indicate rhymes and non-rhymes, with the first line of a poem being a, and the second being a or b according to whether it rhymes with the first line or not.

Here are some familiar traditional rhyme schemes:

The ballad: abcb

The limerick: aabba

The 'Habbie' stanza often used by Burns: aaabab

The Shakespearean Sonnet: abab cdcd efefgg

My mistress' eyes are nothing like the **sun**;	a
Coral is far more red than her lips' **red**;	b
If snow be white, why then her breasts are **dun**;	a
If hairs be wires, black wires grow on her **head**.	b
I have seen roses damask'd, red and **white**,	c
But no such roses see I in her **cheeks**;	d
And in some perfumes is there more **delight**	c
Than in the breath that from my mistress **reeks**.	d
I love to hear her speak, yet well I **know**	e
That music hath a far more pleasing **sound**;	f
I grant I never saw a goddess **go**;	e
My mistress, when she walks, treads on the **ground**:	f
And yet, by heaven, I think my love as **rare**	g
As any she belied with false **compare**.	g

William Shakespeare, 'Sonnet 130'

Rhythm	The sense of 'movement' conveyed by the arrangement of stressed and unstressed syllables. The rhythm in the following poem is very obvious – say it aloud and you'll notice the four stressed syllables (or beats) in the first and third lines of each verse and the three stressed syllables in the second and fourth lines.

A slumber did my spirit steal;

I had no human fears:

She seemed a thing that could not feel

The touch of earthly years.

No motion has she now, no force;

She neither hears nor sees;

Rolled round in earth's diurnal course,

With rocks, and stones, and trees.

William Wordsworth, 'A Slumber Did My Spirit Steal'

Simile	A comparison introduced by words such as 'like' or 'as'.
	Closed like confessionals, they thread Loud noons of cities, giving back None of the glances they absorb. Philip Larkin, 'Ambulances'
Sonnet	A 14-line poem in one of the following forms: • the Italian sonnet, which consists of 8 lines (the octave) rhyming *abbaabba*, and six lines (the sestet), rhyming *cdecde* or *cdccdc* or *cdedce* • the English (or Shakespearean) sonnet, which consists of three quatrains of four lines and a concluding rhyming couplet (*abab cdcd efef gg*) A sonnet is usually written in iambic pentameter – each line contains ten syllables divided into five metric 'feet'. Each 'foot' consists of an unstressed syllable followed by a stressed syllable.
Stanza	Lines of poetry grouped together. Usually any pattern is repeated in following stanzas.
Stress	Emphasis put on a syllable or a word.
Symbol	Something that stands for or represents something. It is clear that 'The Sick Rose' by William Blake is not really a poem about a plant! Instead Blake uses the symbol of the rose to stand for something innocent or beautiful that is being corrupted. O Rose, thou art sick. The invisible worm That flies in the night In the howling storm Has found out thy bed Of crimson joy, And his dark secret love Does thy life destroy. William Blake, 'The Sick Rose'
Theme	The central concern or idea behind a poem.
Tone	The general mood of a poem and how the poet has signalled it to the reader.

Asking questions about poems

Now look at the following selection of poems. After you read each one ask yourself the following questions. Suggested answers for the first two poems are given on pages 123–125.

1. What is the poem about?
2. Who is speaking?
3. How is the poem structured?
4. What other techniques have been used?
5. How effective are the poet's methods in conveying the meaning of the text to the reader?
6. What is your personal reaction to the poem?

Heliographer

I thought we were sitting in the sky.
My father decoded the world beneath:
our tenement, the rival football grounds,
the long bridges, slung out across the river.
Then I gave myself a fright
with the lemonade bottle. Clunk –
the glass thread butting my teeth
as I bolted my mouth to the lip.

Naw ... copy me. It's how the grown-ups drink.
Propped in my shaky,
single-handed grip, I tilted the bottle towards the sun
until it detonated with light,
my lips pursed like a trumpeter's.

Don Paterson

In a snug room

He sips from his glass, thinking complacently
of the events of the day:
a flattering reference to him in the morning papers,
lunch with his cronies, a profitable deal
signed on the dotted line, a donation sent
to his favourite charity.

And he smiles,
thinking of the taxi coming
with his true love in it.
Everything's fine.
And Nemesis slips two bullets
into her gun
in case she misses with the first one

Norman MacCaig

Stopping by Woods on a Snowy Evening

Whose woods these are I think I know.
His house is in the village though;
He will not see me stopping here
To watch his woods fill up with snow.

My little horse must think it queer
To stop without a farmhouse near
Between the woods and frozen lake
The darkest evening of the year.

He gives his harness bells a shake
To ask if there is some mistake.
The only other sound's the sweep
Of easy wind and downy flake.

The woods are lovely, dark and deep.
But I have promises to keep,
And miles to go before I sleep,
And miles to go before I sleep.

Robert Frost

Sonnet 18

Shall I compare thee to a summer's day?
Thou art more lovely and more temperate.
Rough winds do shake the darling buds of May,
And summer's lease hath all too short a date.
Sometime too hot the eye of heaven shines,
And often is his gold complexion dimmed;
And every fair from fair sometime declines,
By chance, or nature's changing course, untrimmed;
But thy eternal summer shall not fade,
Nor lose possession of that fair thou ow'st,
Nor shall death brag thou wand'rest in his shade,
When in eternal lines to Time thou grow'st.
So long as men can breathe, or eyes can see,
So long lives this, and this gives life to thee.

William Shakespeare

Head of English

Today we have a poet in the class.
A real live poet with a published book.
Notice the inkstained fingers girls. Perhaps
we're going to witness verse hot from the press.
Who knows. Please show your appreciation
by clapping. Not too loud. Now

sit up straight and listen. Remember
the lesson on assonance, for not all poems,
sadly rhyme these days. Still. Never mind.
Whispering's as always, out of bounds –
but do feel free to raise some questions.
After all, we're paying forty pounds.

Those of you with English Second Language
see me after break. We're fortunate
to have this person in our midst.
Seasons of mist and so on and so forth.
I've written quite a bit of poetry myself,
am doing Kipling with the Lower Fourth.

Right. That's enough from me. On with the Muse.
Open a window at the back. We don't
want winds of change about this place.
Take notes, but don't write reams. Just an essay
on the poet's themes. Fine. Off we go.
Convince us that there's something we don't know.

Well. Really. Run along now girls. I'm sure
that gave you an insight to an outside view.
Applause will do. Thank you
very much for coming here today. Lunch
in the hall? Do hang about. Unfortunately
I have to dash. Tracey will show you out.

Carol Ann Duffy

Thrushes

Terrifying are the sleek thrushes on the lawn,
More coiled steel than living – a poised
Dark deadly eye, those delicate legs
Triggered to stirrings beyond sense – with a start a bounce, a stab
Overtake the instant and drag out some writhing thing.
No indolent procrastinations and no yawning states,
No sighs or head-scratchings. Nothing but bounce and stab
And a ravening second.

Is it their single-mind-sized skulls or a trained
Body, or genius, or a nestful of brats
Gives their days this bullet and automatic
Purpose? Mozart's brain had it, and the shark's mouth
That hungers down the blood-smell even to a leak of its own
Side and devouring of itself: efficiency which
Strikes too streamlined for any doubt to pluck at it
Or obstruction deflect.

With a man it is otherwise. Heroisms on horseback,
Outstripping his desk-diary at a broad desk,
Carving at a tiny ivory ornament
For years: his act worships itself – while for him,
Though he bends to be blent in the prayer, how
loud and above what
Furious spaces of fire do the distracting devils
Orgy and hossanah, under the wilderness
Of black silent waters weep.

Ted Hughes

Waterfall

The burn drowns steadily in its own downpour,
A helter-skelter of muslin and glass
That skids to a halt, crashing up suds.

Simultaneous acceleration
And sudden braking; water goes over
Like villains dropped screaming to justice.

It appears an athletic glacier
Has reared into reverse: is swallowed up
And regurgitated through this long throat.

My eye rides over and downwards, falls with
Hurtling tons that slabber and spill, Falls, yet
records the tumult thus standing still.

Seamus Heaney

How to study drama

The first thing to remember when analysing a drama text is that it is something that has been created to be performed. Although a play has much in common with a novel in terms of characterisation, theme etc. it is a very different kind of text and the best critical essays will recognise this.

Stage directions offer you vital information about how the play is to be presented to the audience and also provide you with an insight into the central concerns that the dramatist is exploring. If you are dealing with a play by Shakespeare, the stage directions will be minimal. In a modern play, they may be far more detailed as the following examples from Arthur Miller's *All My Sons* show. The extracts are taken from the beginning of act one.

The back yard of the Keller home in the outskirts of an American town. August of our era.

The stage is hedged on right and left by tall, closely planted poplars which lend the yard a secluded atmosphere. Upstage is filled with the back of the house and its open, unroofed porch, which extends into the yard some six feet. The house is two storeys high and has seven rooms. It would have cost perhaps fifteen thousand in the early twenties when it was built. Now it is nicely painted, looks tight and comfortable, and the yard is green with sod, here and there plants whose season is gone. At the right, beside the house, the entrance of the driveway can be seen, but the poplars cut off view of its continuation downstage. In the left corner, downstage, stands the four-foot-high stump of a slender apple tree whose upper trunk and branches lie toppled beside it, fruit still clinging to its branches.

These stage directions at once inform us of the setting in time and place ('an American town' suggests the universality of what will unfold). The apple tree reduced to a stump is an important symbol in the play.

Miller's stage directions also give us a very clear idea of the central character, Joe Keller, from the outset.

Keller is nearing sixty. A heavy man of stolid mind and build, a businessman these many years, but with the imprint of the machine-shop worker and boss still upon him. When he reads, when he speaks, when he listens, it is with the terrible concentration of the uneducated man for whom there is still wonder in many commonly known things. A man whose judgements must be dredged out of experience and a peasant-like common sense. A man among men.

Chapter 2: Literary study

Of course it is not only through stage directions that we learn about the characters. What they do (their actions), what they say, and how they interact with other characters all suggest to the audience how the dramatist intends us to regard them and you should pay close attention to all of these when you are studying the text. Look out for techniques such as **soliloquy** when a character's innermost thoughts and feelings are revealed to the audience. In the following example, Shakespeare ensures the audience is made aware of Iago's plans:

> Cassio's a proper man: let me see now;
> To get his place and to plume up my will
> In double knavery. How? How? Let's see.
> After some time, to abuse Othello's ear
> That he is too familiar with his wife;
> He hath a person and a smooth dispose
> To be suspected, framed to make women false.
> The Moor is of a free and open nature,
> That thinks men honest that but seem to be so,
> And will as tenderly be led by th'nose
> As asses are.
> I have't. It is engendered. Hell and night
> Must bring this monstrous birth to the world's light.
>
> *Othello I.3.386–398*

Pay close attention to how a character develops and changes during the course of the play. Does your response to a character change as the action unfolds? Does the character match the definition of any common dramatic types, e.g. the tragic hero, whose downfall is the result of some flaw in their character?

Relationships are usually at the heart of any play. Look at how the dramatist presents them to the audience and how they are used to explore the central concerns of the play. Consider the use of **dialogue**. Is it **naturalistic** or are some speeches clearly meant to have **symbolic** significance? Look at how lighting and other staging techniques help to give prominence to some speeches. Find the lines that seem to encapsulate the central concerns of the play.

Look carefully at how the play is structured. The Ancient Greeks thought that tragedy should follow the following pattern: *exposition* (or introduction); *rising action* (or complication); *crisis* (some sort of turning point); *falling action* (showing the forces operating against the hero); *catastrophe* (usually the death of the tragic hero). However, not all tragedies fit neatly into this pattern. Many modern plays have a much looser structure than the five acts of Shakespeare's tragedies, but you should still be able to spot **key scenes**, **turning points** and the **climax** of the action. Another technical term you should be able to use is **dénouement**. This refers to the part of the play when the outcome is revealed to the audience. How do you react to this?

Finally, consider what you think the dramatist's message is for the audience. What are the central concerns or themes of the play? How effective are the various dramatic techniques used in helping to convey these themes?

Reading for understanding, analysis and evaluation

As we've already discussed in the course outline and assessment section at the start of this book, Reading in the Higher English course is assessed in two different ways.

The internal assessment requires you to answer a series of questions on a text that you have not seen before.

The external assessment (the SQA examination) requires you to take on:

'the challenge of applying reading skills, understanding, analysis and evaluation to two non-fiction texts. Assessment tasks will involve learners answering questions to show their understanding, analysis and evaluation of non-fiction texts and summarising information for a purpose.' (SQA, 2013)

This means that the Reading for Understanding, Analysis and Evaluation examination paper requires the additional skills of comparing and contrasting two different passages.

Understanding, analysis, evaluation

The sorts of questions you can expect in the examination paper fall into the following categories.

1. Questions that test your **understanding** of the writer's ideas (*what* the writer is trying to say). These tend to be the more straightforward questions in the examination.

2. Questions that test your skills of **analysis**. You will be asked to explain the techniques used by the writer (*how* the writer conveys his or her message). You will be asked to explain how the writer's use of language (which might include such things as word choice, imagery, sentence structure, sound, tone imagery and structure) helps to get across their point of view. You will also be asked how these techniques add to the impact of the passage.

3. Questions that ask you to **evaluate** how successful the writer is in using particular techniques or how effective they are in achieving the purpose of the writing.

TOP TIP

Each question will have a number of marks attached to it. Questions will be worth between **2** and **5** marks. The number of marks allocated to a question is generally a good guide to the length of answer required from you. A 2-mark question asking you to identify two basic points made in the passage will require a more concise answer than a 4-mark question which asks you to analyse a range of language features. Obviously you have to answer the question but don't waste time writing unnecessarily long answers – this is after all a test of your reading, not your writing. The 5-mark question asking you to identify key areas from both passages can be answered either in a series of bullet points or in a number of linked sentences – we'll look at this particular question in more detail later. Above all, you need to use the **1 hour and 30 minutes** you have to complete this paper as efficiently as you can; make sure you answer **all** the questions.

Passages

Passages for the reading for understanding, analysis and evaluation paper are always non-fiction.

This means that they could, for example, be taken from things like:

- a newspaper article
- a magazine article
- a popular science book
- a biography
- a piece of travel writing
- a report.

Passages might come from traditional print or online texts.

In order to get yourself familiar with the sort of writing found in these passages you could look at the SQA specimen paper and also the *Higher Practice Papers for SQA Exams* produced by *Leckie & Leckie*.

You should also seek out this kind of writing for yourself. Feature articles in newspapers such as *The Times, The Herald, The Guardian, The Telegraph, The Scotsman, The Independent* and their Sunday equivalents will all include examples of the kind of writing chosen for exam passages. You can access most of these online. Pay particular attention to articles written by a newspaper's regular columnists – these are likely to contain good examples of persuasive and argumentative writing.

There are also any number of blogs online that will provide you with appropriate reading material which might be useful for practice. Look out for reputable print or TV journalists who also write blogs. Following newspapers and journalists on Twitter will usually supply you with links to longer written pieces.

TOP TIP

Your school librarian will be of invaluable assistance in suggesting the 'right' sort of reading. Make a point of talking to them – they will only be too delighted to assist you.

TOP TIP

Once you've started finding examples of the kinds of passages used in the exam, practise making up questions on them. Thinking *'What might I be asked about this part of the passage?'* is an excellent way of making yourself really focus on the language techniques used by a writer.

Types of questions: understanding

If you have already done National 5 English, you will already be familiar with some of the things that you will be asked at Higher. Let's look at some examples of questions that you might find in a Higher paper.

Questions that test your understanding

Referring to lines 8–11, identify **two** ways in which 'our prison system is not fit for purpose'.

Read lines 22–33. According to the writer in lines 24–26, in what ways are online shoppers different to those who shop on the High Street?

Explain in detail why the writer thinks that women 'can never achieve full equality' (line 31).

Explain the cause of the 'pessimism' expressed by the economist (line 4).

Explain why the writer does not believe that 'humanity's journey has a positive destination' (line 15).

Re-read lines 50–55. Identify any four reasons given in these lines for abandoning the wave power project.

According to lines 43–47, why does the writer believe 'our online identities are merely artificial constructs'?

Notice that you are always told where to look for the answer in the passage with a reference to the line number(s). Key words in this category of question are often words and phrases like **explain**, **give reasons for**, **according to the writer what is …**, **why**, **identify**.

For all questions that test your understanding, you **must** attempt to answer in your own words as far as possible. You **must not** simply copy down the words of the passage.
Remember that you are not always reminded of this requirement in individual questions at Higher. There is an assumption that you will answer questions using your own words (there are, of course, questions that do require you to quote from the passage as part of your answer but these are dealt with below). Identifying and explaining the ideas of a passage is not only a test of your ability to understand these ideas, it is also a test of your vocabulary. That is why it is so important you read as widely as possible during this course.

TOP TIP

If you are asked to 'identify' something in the passage, simply supply the answer in a concise form or name.

Locate, translate

As a first step in answering this kind of question you should first of all **locate** the part of the passage that will supply you with the answer and underline or highlight it – remember that the exam paper is for you to use as you like – and then **translate** it into your own words. If you can't remember **locate, translate**, then think about the following commands in your computer's word processing software:

FIND [ ]

REPLACE WITH [ ]

Let's see how that works in practice.

Look at the following extract from Ed Smith's book, *What Sport Tells Us About Life*. It is taken from a chapter that discusses the concept of 'amateurism'. Then look at the question which follows it.

One generation's favourite idea is despised by the next as old-fashioned rubbish. That is what happened to amateurism.

At its peak, the character-building philosophy of amateurism defined British attitudes to sport. A century ago 'amateur' was a compliment to someone who played sport simply for the love of it – it is derived, after all, from the Latin for 'to love'. The word professional, on the other hand, scarcely existed as a noun.

How the wheel has turned. In fact, the words have almost completely swapped meanings. 'Professional' now has a definition so broad that almost anyone who has held down a job for a few months can call himself a 'true professional'. And amateurism has become a byword for sloppiness, disorganisation and ineptitude.

Question: According to the writer, what are the current meanings of the words 'professional' and 'amateur'?

2

The first thing to do is to **locate** the parts of the passage that will supply us with the answer. Remember you will find it helpful to <u>underline</u> or highlight the appropriate words.

One generation's favourite idea is despised by the next as old-fashioned rubbish. That is what happened to amateurism.

At its peak, the character-building philosophy of amateurism defined British attitudes to sport. A century ago 'amateur' was a compliment to someone who played sport simply for the love of it – it is derived, after all, from the Latin for 'to love'. The word professional, on the other hand, scarcely existed as a noun.

How the wheel has turned. In fact, the words have almost completely swapped meanings. 'Professional' now has a definition so broad that almost anyone who has held down a job for a few months can call himself a 'true professional'. And amateurism has become a byword for sloppiness, disorganisation and ineptitude.

The next step is simply to **translate** or paraphrase the highlighted or underlined text into your own words.

Answer: It's hard to say exactly what 'professional' means as so many people regard themselves as one and 'amateurism' has become another name or label for poor performance.

TOP TIP

Remember you can mark up or highlight the exam paper in any way that you find helpful.

This answer shows that the appropriate parts of the passage have been identified and that the writer's words have been successfully **glossed** by the candidate.

Remember you are dealing with 'detailed and complex' language at Higher level so you are always likely to come across words with which you might be unfamiliar. When this happens, don't just give up. Use the following tactics:

Look at the rest of the sentence and the other sentences immediately before and after the word again – **the context**. This might give you some idea of a possible meaning.

Words are made up of **roots** and **stems**. Are there any clues there? For example, if you didn't know what the word 'laudable' meant you might still be reminded of the word 'applaud' and so be able to work out that 'laudable' means 'praiseworthy'.

Is there another word, or phrase, close to the word, that appears to have a similar meaning?

Is there another word or phrase, close to the word, that suggests the opposite meaning? Is the writer trying to indicate a contrast of some kind?

Does the writer make use of an example that might help to explain the meaning of the word?

Above all, don't get thrown by the unfamiliar – try to work it out as best you can.

Now practise using what you have learned to answer a selection of questions on the rest of the extract from Ed Smith's book. Check your answers on page 125. The questions all test your **understanding**. In the exam there will probably be a maximum of three 2-mark questions.

The age of the amateur has passed

Worse luck

One generation's favourite idea is despised by the next as old-fashioned rubbish. That is what happened to amateurism.

At its peak, the character-building philosophy of amateurism defined British attitudes to sport. A century ago 'amateur' was a compliment to someone who
5 played sport simply for the love of it – it is derived, after all, from the Latin for 'to love'. The word professional, on the other hand, scarcely existed as a noun.

How the wheel has turned. In fact, the words have almost completely swapped meanings. 'Professional' now has a definition so broad that almost anyone who has held down a job for a few months can call himself a 'true professional'. And
10 amateurism has become a byword for sloppiness, disorganisation and ineptitude.

'The amateur, formerly the symbol of fair play and a stout heart,' as the literary critic D.J. Taylor put it, 'became the watchword for terminal second-rateness and lower-rung incompetence.' Have we thrown the baby out with the bathwater?

There is no doubt that the survival of amateur rhetoric so far into the twentieth
15 century was a bizarre anachronism, even by British standards. When Fred Titmus made his debut for Middlesex at cricket in 1949, his progress to the wicket was accompanied by a loudspeaker announcement correcting an error on the score-card: 'F.J. Titmus should, of course, read Titmus, F.J.' A gentleman was allowed his initial before the surname; a professional's came after. People felt these things
20 mattered.

There are countless stories about grand but hopeless amateurs insisting that far more talented pros call them 'Mr' – even on the field of play.

Clearly the amateur ideal – in its snobbery, exclusivity and sometimes plain silliness – assisted in its own demise. But now professionalism has had a good
25 crack of the whip, perhaps it is time we drew stock about where that ideal has taken us. And as we wave amateurism goodbye, could there be anything in its wreckage that might be worth salvaging?

First of all, we might consider whether amateurism allowed for a broad church of personalities, and encouraged an instinctiveness and individuality that is well
30 suited to producing success in sport. Secondly, perhaps amateurism left people alone more – and it might be that great players respond well to being left alone.

It is a truism that there is a creative element to the best sport. We crave creative midfield footballers, creative managers and creative leadership. Alongside their creativity, sportsmen are often lauded when they seem inspired – we talk of an
35 inspired spell of bowling, an inspired tactical move or an inspirational act of defiance. The language of sporting excellence draws heavily from the arts – for the very good reason that playing sport has much in common with artistic expression.

What do we mean when we talk of creativity and inspiration? Perhaps we can never fully understand the answer. Many of the most inspired sporting
40 achievements, like great works of art or innovation, spring from parts of our personalities which resist rational analysis, let alone professional planning. Where does a writer find inspiration for a novel? Where do scientific ideas come from,

how does an entrepreneur come up with a new business idea? There will be
an element of self-awareness in all these processes – a management of talent,
45 a regulation of originality – but also a good amount of instinct. Forces beyond
rationality lead creative people to follow certain paths and not others. Like strikers
with an instinct for where to be in the penalty area, something takes them into
different (and better) creative territory.

Crucially, the wisest of these original minds
50 know better than to over-analyse the sources of
their inspiration. They do not undermine the
muse by trying to master her. Whatever works
should be left well alone. 'If the word "inspiration"
is to have any meaning,' wrote T.S. Eliot, 'it must
55 mean that the speaker or writer is uttering
something which he does not wholly understand –
or which he may even misinterpret when the
inspiration has departed from him.' After all,
'inspiration' derives linguistically from the
60 concept of breath – once breathed out it is gone.

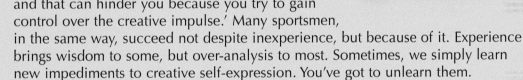

Bob Dylan has argued that inspiration needs
to be protected from too much 'grown-up'
self-analysis: 'As you get older, you get smarter
and that can hinder you because you try to gain
65 control over the creative impulse.' Many sportsmen,
in the same way, succeed not despite inexperience, but because of it. Experience
brings wisdom to some, but over-analysis to most. Sometimes, we simply learn
new impediments to creative self-expression. You've got to unlearn them.

Ed Smith, *What Sport Tells Us About Life*

Questions

		Marks
1.	Re-read lines 1–2. According to the writer, what 'has happened to amateurism'?	2
2.	Re-read lines 14–22. Identify **two** examples of what the writer terms 'bizarre anachronism'.	2
3.	Re-read lines 28–31. According to the writer, what were two possible advantages of amateurism?	2
4.	Re-read lines 38–48. According to the writer, what do 'many of the most inspired sporting achievements' have in common with 'great works of art or innovation'?	2
5.	Re-read lines 61–68. According to the writer, what makes many sportsmen successful?	2

Check your answers on pages 128–131.

Types of questions: analysis

Analysis questions

Questions that test your skills of **analysis** are generally more challenging. Here is a selection.

> Analyse how the writer's use of language in lines 10–15 emphasises her dislike of celebrity culture. You should refer in your answer to such features as sentence structure, word choice, imagery, contrast, tone...
>
> Re-read lines 22–28. By referring to at least two examples, analyse how the writer's use of imagery highlights the contrast between rural and urban communities.
>
> By referring to at least two features of language in lines 17–27 analyse how the writer conveys his attitude towards social media. You should refer in your answer to such features as sentence structure, word choice, contrast, tone...
>
> Re-read lines 7–17. By referring to at least two features of language in lines 21–17, analyse how the writer conveys the seriousness of the situation faced by the journalists.

Notice that the key word in all these questions is **analyse**.

Other key words in this type of question are the technical terms **word choice**, **language**, **tone**, **sentence structure**, **imagery**. Sometimes the question will remind you that these are the techniques to analyse, sometimes the question will just use the term **features of language**. As soon as you see this term, a checklist should start running automatically in your head: word choice, imagery, sentence structure, sound, tone, punctuation ...

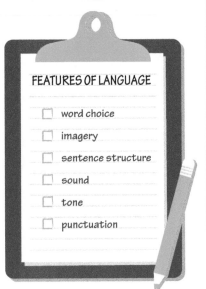

FEATURES OF LANGUAGE

- [ ] word choice
- [ ] imagery
- [ ] sentence structure
- [ ] sound
- [ ] tone
- [ ] punctuation

In order to answer questions that require you to analyse the writer's use of language features, the first thing you must do is to refer to the technique(s) being used by the author (usually accompanied by quotation). Unfortunately, there are no marks for this part of your answer. The second thing you must do is comment on how the particular technique is used. The marks are awarded for your comments. An appropriate reference to a language feature and a detailed or insightful comment will usually get you 2 marks; a reference plus a more basic comment will be worth 1.

Let's see how that works in practice.

Read the following extract from an article by music journalist Alexis Petridis on youth subcultures and the question that follows.

I'm trying to investigate the state of youth subcultures in 2014. It seems a worthwhile thing to do. You hardly need a degree in sociology to realise that something fairly dramatic has happened to them over the past couple of decades; you just need a functioning pair of eyes. When I arrived at secondary school in the mid-80s, the fifth and sixth forms, where uniform requirements were relaxed, looked like a mass of different tribes, all of them defined by the music they liked, all of them more or less wearing their tastes on their sleeves. There were goths. There were metallers. There were punks. There were soulboys, at least one of whom had made the fateful decision to try and complete his look by growing a moustache, the bum fluff result pathetic in the extreme. There were Morrissey acolytes, and even a couple of ersatz hippies, one of whom had decorated his Adidas holdall with a drawing of the complex front cover of Gong's 1971 album *Camembert Electrique*: a pretty ballsy move, given the derision that hippies had suffered during punk, and at the hands of the scriptwriters of *The Young Ones*.

From an article by Alex Petridis in *The Guardian*, Thursday 20 March 2014

Question: Analyse how the writer's use of language emphasises the wide variety of youth subcultures the writer encountered when he was at school. You should refer in your answer to such features as sentence structure, word choice, imagery, contrast, tone...　　**2**

To answer this question, look for appropriate language features, quote/refer to them and then comment on their connotations. Your answer should include at least two of the following:

Word choice

'*mass*' suggests a large number.

'*different tribes*' suggests assorted, almost primitive, groups.

Sentence structure

Repetition. '*There were ... There were ...*' emphasises the number of different groups.

Listing. '*goths ... metallers ... punks ... soulboys*' indicates the range of subcultures.

Short sentences. '*There were goths. There were metallers.*' highlights that each group was separate from the others.

Let's look at how to deal with each language feature in more detail.

To comment on **word choice** simply quote the appropriate word (or words) and comment on the **connotations** of that word. In other words make sure you say what that word **suggests** rather than just what it **means**. Remember that the writer will have chosen that particular word carefully for the specific effect it will create.

Answers on word choice can be written very economically and effectively like this:

Word　　　　　suggests　　　　　　reference to connotations/effect of word

For example:

'*sunset*' suggests something coming to an end/death.

'*thorny*' suggests something difficult or painful to deal with.

'rationale' *suggests a more sophisticated reason/things have been thought through logically.*

'maternal' *suggests a caring attitude.*

'pedestrian' *suggests something very ordinary.*

Now let us consider questions about imagery.

An image is just a picture in words. In the kind of non-fiction writing used in the reading for understanding, analysis and evaluation exam paper, a writer will use imagery to help illustrate a point being made or to achieve a particular effect.

Look at how the nature writer Mark Cocker describes a flock of crows.

> It is no longer a flock of birds. Each occasion I see these protean swirls rise they act like ink-blot tests drawing images out of my unconscious. Sometimes they seem like something you saw before you left the womb, before your eyes first opened, an entopic vision buried deep beneath the avalanche of waking experience: black dust motes sinking steadily through the gentle oil of sleep. Tonight the flock blossoms as an immense night flower and, while beautiful and mysterious, it always stirs something edgy into my sense of wonder. It is the feeling that in viewing the unnumbered and unnumberable birds, I am tipped towards the state of confusion which that inchoate twisting swerve so perfectly represents.
>
> Mark Cocker, *Crow Country*

Here is one way to answer questions on imagery (your teacher/tutor might suggest other equally valid approaches). First of all explain the 'root' of the image and say what is being compared with what. Think about what the two things have in common and what the writer is suggesting by making this comparison. Then go on to say why this makes the image effective or otherwise.

You might be asked the following question about imagery:

Question: By referring to at least one example, analyse how the writer's use of imagery conveys his experience of watching crows.

To answer this question, find the images used by the writer, explain the 'root' of these images and go on to comment on what they suggest about the experience.

A possible answer might look like this:

The writer compares watching a flock of crows to undergoing an 'ink-blot' test. Depending on what we see in them, ink-blot tests are designed to reveal things in our subconscious and the writer's use of this simile effectively suggests the many different patterns formed by the crows and the deep and powerful effect watching them has on him.

Now see if you can comment in the same way on:

- like something you saw before you left the womb
- an entopic vision buried deep beneath the avalanche of waking experience
- black dust motes sinking steadily through the gentle oil of sleep
- the flock blossoms as an immense night flower.

> ## TOP TIP
> Make sure you are able to identify techniques such as simile, metaphor and personification so that you can respond effectively to questions on imagery.

Types of questions: analysing sentences – structure and punctuation

Sometimes a question will ask you directly about sentence structure and/or punctuation but don't forget to consider these if the question asks about the writer's use of **language**.

In answering questions on sentence structure and punctuation you must identify the technique that is being used and then comment on what effect it has. As always, there are no marks awarded for the reference you make – for example, you get nothing for pointing out that

> *The writer uses a list in line 55.*

Marks are allocated depending on the quality of your **comment** on the effect of the list. Structure your answer by referring first of all to the technique and then adding your comment.

> *The list in line 55 ('the carefree, the careworn, the innocent, the guilty, the indolent, the industrious ...') suggests the wide variety of personalities in the room.*

Any time you are asked about sentence structure, a checklist of possible features should start running in your head.

Ask yourself, is it a long sentence? A short sentence? A list …?

Once you've spotted the technique, think about the effect it creates. The following table gives you a reminder of different sentence features and their effects.

Feature — types of sentence	Possible effects
Statement	• conveying facts • making assertions
Question	• involves the reader • indicates writer reflecting on or considering things • a series of questions might suggest bewilderment/puzzlement
Rhetorical question	• invites the reader to think • invites the reader to share the writer's opinion
Exclamation	• expresses emotion (surprise, anger etc.)
Command (imperative)	• instructions • can suggest friendly informality (*Bring a friend …; Imagine you are …*)
Minor sentence	• impact • informality • suspense
Sentence in a paragraph of its own	• impact • drama

Feature — structure	Possible effects
Long sentence	To describe (amongst other things): • physical length • a complex process • a series of activities • something tedious or boring
Short sentence	• (dramatic) impact
List	• number of examples • reinforcement of an idea • range or variety
Repetition	• emphasis (always say **what** it emphasises)

Inversion	• changes focus/emphasis of the sentence to the displaced word(s)
Climax	• builds up to something (say **what** that is)
Anti-climax	• builds up and then descends to something contrasting with what has gone before (often used for humorous effect)
Antithesis	• contrasting ideas (look at **what** is being contrasted and why)

Feature — punctuation	Possible effects
Capitalisation	indicates • names • titles • significance
Inverted commas '...'	indicate • names • titles • direct speech • quotation • writer using word ironically
Comma ,	separates • clauses • items in a list
Colon :	introduces • a list • an expansion of an idea • quotation
Semi-colon ;	• 'hinge' in a balanced sentence • separates phrasal items in a list
Dash –	• introduces an explanation or expansion of an idea • introduces an aside or afterthought from the writer
Parenthesis – – or ( ) or , ,	indicates extra information included in the sentence (remember that you must comment on **what** the extra information **adds** to the sentence)
ellipsis ...	• indicates words missing • suggests a list could continue • interruption • hesitation

Here is an extract from an article on teenagers and their parents by the journalist Suzanne Moore. Look at it and try to explain what effects are achieved by the writer's use of sentence structure.

'Your child is going to experiment': what teenagers really think

It's so unfair. No one understands you. People who actually have no idea tell you what to do all the time. About anything. Everyone patronises you or exchanges knowing looks when you say something really important. No one sees you as an individual any more but just as some kind of generic blob. No one is there when you feel really lonely. No one is there when you discover something completely weird about the world. No one is there when you are too tired to pick up the remote control. No one gets quite how boring all of this is.

This is how it feels to be the parent of a teenager. Not all the time. Some of the time. I can't tell you how to do it, but I can reassure you that you are probably doing it *all* wrong. There are experts in adolescence, apparently. There are manuals that are fine if you accept that you just need to change the settings on teenagers until their lights flash on and off. Teenagers are bracketed with toddlers in terms of targeted user guides. This seems naff, but there is no one these days apparently not in need of some dumbed-down cognitive behavioural therapy. Strangely, I happen to believe teenagers – er, much like us grown-ups – are all different.

I am currently on my third teenager (she is 13; my older ones are in their 20s), but the real truth is that I am on my fourth. Me! I was a teenager. It is this experience more than anything that informs my parenting. For I know I was pretty much formed as a person by 14, and I haven't changed that much since. That may be a good thing or a bad thing. Your relationship to your adolescent is often hooked into the relationship you have with your own adolescence. So many irrational fears, hopes and denials come from this nowhere land.

That's why, when your child starts the journey of separating from you, you may react in all sorts of strange ways. You as a parent may feel suddenly out of control. Of yourself as well as of your child.

Many people seem anxious that what is seen as adolescent behaviour kicks in long before the teen years, at about 10. By this I mean the stereotypical way that we define this phase: wanting stuff, being sarcastic, needing to be alone sometimes, caring too much about being included or excluded from particular groups, demanding the impossible, being oversensitive, easily hurt and inexplicably angry. All the while doing daft things. None of these behaviours belongs to any one age group, but we tend to see teenagers' emotional lives as somehow always excessive and exaggerated.

From an article by Suzanne Moore in *The Guardian*, Thursday 14 June 2014

You should have spotted:

- the short emphatic statement at the start of the passage, 'It's so unfair' to introduce the writer's complaints
- the use of the minor sentence 'About anything' to bluntly reinforce the sense of unfairness
- the repetition of 'No one … No one …' to effectively suggest the sense of the writer's feelings of isolation/lack of empathy from others
- the use of parenthesis ' – er, much like us grown-ups –' to add a conversational aside that acknowledges what the two groups have in common
- the use of the colon to introduce a list of stereotypical teenage behaviours
- the use of 'but' in 'None of these behaviours …, but we tend to see …' to indicate the contrast between reality and our perception of teenage behaviour.

Did you spot any other features?

Tone

Tone is sometimes a difficult thing to identify in a piece of writing. It's much easier to spot when someone is talking to you. You immediately know for example if the person is angry, bitter or enthusiastic. We can all usually tell when someone is being sarcastic ('Yeah, Higher English is so easy.') The tone someone uses when speaking reveals their attitude to what they are saying.

It's the same in writing. The tone a writer adopts will reflect his or her attitude to their subject matter.

You need to be able to identify when a writer is being ironic or nostalgic or angry or serious or enthusiastic or humorous or…

When you are faced with a question in the Close Reading paper which asks you to 'Comment on the writer's tone…' you must first identify which tone you think the writer has adopted and go on to explain how the language features used help to establish the tone. Look at how the writer uses techniques such as word choice, imagery and sentence structure to suggest this tone.

> **TOP TIP**
>
> Don't say the writer is being sarcastic unless you are absolutely certain of this. Too many candidates use this as a kind of automatic response to questions about tone!

Try this

Read the extracts on the next two pages by *Guardian* journalist, Lucy Mangan. They are from an article in which she discusses the novel *Twilight* and the film of the same name.

Look at the highlighted pieces of text and try to explain how they contribute to the **critical** tone she adopts (it's clear she's not a fan). The first section has been done for you.

See if you agree with the comments at the end of this chapter on pages 52–53.

> **TOP TIP**
>
> Always look carefully at the information given to you about each passage in the exam. It can sometimes give you a clue to the overall tone of the passage.

Dangerous liaisons

As most teenage girls in Britain will already know, Twilight – a tale of love between a young woman and a vampire – has now been made into a movie. It will no doubt be a huge hit. But what a shame it's not more like Buffy, writes Lucy Mangan

Twilight premiered last night. If you don't know what that means, the chances are that you are neither a teenage girl nor mother or teacher of same. If you were, you would know instantly that today is the day the first book in Stephanie Meyer's internationally bestselling vampire romance saga comes to the big screen.

The idea for the book came in a dream, says Meyer, a Mormon who performed the impressive feat of typing the subsequent 500-page narrative one-handed with a baby on her lap and two other children under five playing round her feet.

Looking at the synopsis of *Twilight*, sceptics and cynics might ask if this was a dream that came to the author after she fell asleep in front of an episode of Joss Whedon's television series *Buffy the Vampire Slayer*, which also centred round the relationship between a high school girl and a 'good' vampire who couldn't have sex for fear that he would turn evil again. Sceptics and cynics who have actually read *Twilight* or seen the film, however, will simply roll their eyes at their misguided brethren and say, 'If only.'

If only Meyer had taken Buffy as her template. If only she had used that groundbreaking series as her foundation and built on it. If only there was a Whedonesque intelligence and modern, feminist sensibility informing Twilight and its successors. If only.

You should have spotted:

- the repetition of 'If only …' to highlight the writer's low opinion of Meyer's work compared to Buffy.
- that the minor sentence to end the paragraph adds impact and drives the writer's message home.

Now go on to look at the rest of the article.

What you have instead in Meyer's work is a depressingly retrograde, deeply anti-feminist, borderline misogynistic novel that drains its heroine of life and vitality as surely as if a vampire had sunk his teeth into her and leaves her a bloodless cipher while the story happens around her. Edward tells her she is 'so interesting … fascinating', but the reader looks in vain for his evidence.

Far more important, however, is the nature of the relationship between Bella and Edward. In interviews, Meyer claims that the theme of the *Twilight* saga is choice, because Edward chooses not to behave as his nature impels him to. Alas, the only choice Bella gets to make is to sacrifice herself in ever-larger increments.

It sounds melodramatic and shrill to say that Bella and Edward's relationship is abusive, but as the story wears on it becomes increasingly hard to avoid the comparison, as she gradually isolates herself from her friends to protect his secret, and learns to subordinate her every impulse and movement to the necessity of not upsetting Edward and his instincts.

Edward, of course, has warned her not to be alone with him. To those less enamoured of Meyerworld, the implication is that Bella chooses to put herself in danger and the further implication is that she must therefore bear full responsibility for the consequences (which, in the way of vampire romances, are not entirely confined to hugs and puppies).

In the book (though, naturally, less so in the film, as she is still physically present on screen), despite being the narrator, Bella all but disappears as a character. The few signs of wit and independence she exhibits at the beginning of the book, when she is starting her new school, have long been abandoned in favour of mute devotion to Edward, which by the end is so slavish that she asks him to turn her into a vampire too, so that he needn't be frightened of killing her any more.

Now, teenage readers – or viewers, although the film loses much of the written detail of Bella and Edward's relationship, which in this case could be classed as a good thing – aren't idiots. But they are young, inexperienced and underinformed, and that makes them vulnerable to influences they are exposed to uncritically.

Edward is no hero. Bella is no Buffy. And *Twilight's* underlying message – that self-sacrifice makes you a worthy girlfriend, that men mustn't be excited beyond a certain point, that men with problems must be forgiven everything, that female passivity is a state to be encouraged – are no good to anyone. It should be staked through its black, black heart.

Did you spot any other features which contribute to the critical tone?

Types of questions: evaluation

Evaluation questions ask you to evaluate **how successful** the writer is in using particular techniques or **how effective** he or she has been in achieving the purpose of the writing.

You might be faced with the following:

> **Evaluate how successful** you find the opening paragraph as an introduction to the passage.

When you are asked how effective or how successful something is in the passage it is usually easier to say that you do find it very successful and then comment on how the writer's techniques contribute to this. Don't forget to make your evaluation clear in your answer (I find this very effective because…). However, you **are** allowed to say you **don't** find something particularly effective or successful as long as you support this view with evidence from the passage. It is perfectly acceptable, for example, to argue that you find a particular use of imagery less successful because of its rather clichéd nature. Whichever approach you choose to take, remember to support your comments with reference to appropriate ideas and language features in the passage.

Now try putting your knowledge of language features to the test by reading the following passages on private schools, education jargon and allowing toddlers to play video games. *Identify* and *comment* on:

- word choice
- imagery
- sentence structure
- tone.

Stop criticising private schools, start learning from them

Former Chancellor, Lord Lamont, is absolutely right to say we should take more pride in our private schools, and see them as "great national assets".

Private schools are renowned the world over: a British success story increasingly being exported, with top schools like Cranleigh, Dulwich, Harrow, Marlborough and Wellington, all setting up overseas subsidiaries in the Far and Middle East.

Meanwhile Eton itself, founded in 1440, is a byword in educational achievement. How many other institutions, British or otherwise, have flourished for 574 years?

So why are so many, as Lord Lamont observes, so critical of private schools? Is this pure envy?

Whatever the reason, it's not enough simply to sit back and take pride in these excellent institutions. We need to learn what makes them successful and translate some of the attitudes, some of the culture, to the maintained sector too.

What an irony: Britain has probably the best independent schools in the world; but on the other side of the "Berlin Wall", has a maintained sector increasingly languishing behind our competitors, as the PISA tests revealed.

So what makes private schools special? First and foremost, the "can do" attitude they foster amongst pupils. Success, achievement, ambition, pride: these are not dirty words, to be avoided at all costs, but are embedded in the ethos of all independent schools – often seen in their mottos.

Cheltenham College's is typical: "Labor Omnia Vincit" ("Work Conquers All"). Or how about "Industria", the motto of Tony Blair's alma mater, Fettes College (often regarded as "Scotland's Eton"), exhorting its pupils to work harder.

The fact such mottos are still unashamedly in Latin, itself makes a statement about excellence: "You don't know the meaning? Why not look it up and learn something?"

Apart from "Floreat Etona", "May Eton Flourish" (no shortage of pride there), one of the most famous mottos is Winchester College's "Manners makyth man".

This may sound unfashionable, until you remember that Winchester, founded in 1382, has been around for over 600 years – even predating Eton. Surely that's something to take pride in?

In contrast, every time I pass a comprehensive, I am struck by the bland, meaningless "mission statements" posted proudly outside school gates. Usually these run something along the lines of "excellence for everyone", or "achievement for all", or some such other woolly, waffly, slogan. How exactly is this to be achieved, I find myself wondering?

Next, private schools encourage competition – and not just in the classroom itself, with well-publicised grading systems and form orders, so everyone knows exactly how they stand, but also on the sports field.

Competitive sport is, sadly, on its way out in too many maintained schools. But in the private sector, sport flourishes: with regular rugby, soccer, cricket fixtures. This is why 40 per cent of medals at the London Olympics were won by former private pupils. When will we realise that "competition" too is not taboo?

Crucially, private schools also give every pupil a sense of community and belonging. They achieve this through their "house" systems. No matter how large the school, from two hundred to the huge size of Eton, boys and girls will be split into smaller, friendlier, school houses of fifty or sixty pupils.

Fierce rivalries between houses are engendered; fierce loyalties develop. A strong sense of identity and confidence is the end result.

So let's stop criticising private schools and start learning a few lessons from them for a change.

The author teaches English at a top independent boarding school.

From an article in *The Telegraph*, 29 July 2014

Secret Teacher: jargon is ruining our children's education

Ugly words – such as learning objectives, non-negotiables and targets – are meaningless to young pupils and put too much pressure on them too soon.

"What do you do when you get to school in the morning?" a colleague asked a younger member of my family recently. "Well, when we get to class, we get out our books and start on our non-negotiables," replied the child, who is in year 2. "What are they?" the colleague inquired. "Don't know" was the answer.

This is a perfect example of what is bothering me as a primary school teacher – educational jargon that is passed on to our children. At no point during my own education was I ever aware of non-negotiables, targets, levels, learning objectives or success criteria. But my teachers still taught me a great deal and it was pretty obvious that I was learning. Where I stood in the academic pecking order was the teacher's business, not mine.

But the constant jargon that teachers are forced to use is rubbing off on our students. Not only is this meaningless for them but it's increasingly making their academic performance their responsibility too. Do primary school children really need that kind of pressure when they're so young?

Despite my objections, this year I prepared a group of year 6 children to have a go at the Sats level 6 papers. Level 6 is designed for children aged 14, but these students were very secure at level 5. One girl in particular found this process really difficult and, when I found her in tears after a practice test, it was clear from our conversation that however much I tried to explain that level 6 was miles ahead of where she was supposed to be, it hadn't really sunk in.

"Why are you so upset?" I asked.

"Because I just don't think I'm going to get a level 6 in reading, and that's my target."

"Really? Did I ever tell you that was your target?"

"No, but I'm doing the paper."

"Well, what will happen if you don't get the level 6? What level will you get instead?"

"I'll just get a level 5."

"And do you know what level most children leave primary school with? Level 4b, so it's not just a level 5 – you're already higher than average."

"Oh."

"Just do the best that you can."

"Ok, thanks Miss. And you won't be disappointed if I don't get level 6?"

"No, not at all. If you try your hardest I'll be happy with whatever you get."

By dragging children into a stupid numbers game with us, we do them a great disservice. They don't respond well to the pressure, and levels and targets don't tell the tale of their primary education. But many schools make children believe it really matters. Of course it matters to teachers and management, because that is what we as professionals are judged on, but it is of little consequence to the children themselves.

In the same vein, schools conduct their own type of Pavlov's dog experiment by conditioning students to think that they are only learning when they use the correct buzzwords. Learning that takes place outside of the objective is rarely valued or recognised, and teachers who train under this rigid system never realise there was ever another way.

Learning is apparently pointless unless it has a clear "objective" shared with the children, and children cannot possibly achieve anything unless they follow the success criteria. While these concepts are amazing tools for professionals when used with care and thought, too often the jargon leads to boring teaching. And teachers only feel obliged to cling on to these terms to get approval from other adults.

Children are expected to jump perfectly through adult-designed hoops in other ways too. The question most often asked of children in a lesson observation is: "What you are learning?" Should the child dare to reply by enthusiastically telling the adult about what they are doing, then the teacher is penalised because the learning objective isn't clear enough. For many children, this is an extremely demanding question and one many will not be developmentally ready for. When a child plays with Lego they don't say, "I'm developing my sense of spatial awareness and 3D shapes, as well elementary engineering and architecture." Rather, they say: "Look at the house I built!" Should we really expect them to respond any differently?

Teachers need to claim back their intellectual confidence and decide what is best for their children, exercising professional judgment without fear of criticism. Too much of children's time is wasted telling them in great detail what skills they are developing as if they were able to stand outside of themselves and see the wider application of these skills.

Thankfully I now work in an environment where the management appreciate that learning does not have to take a set format. I don't feel obliged to tick their boxes and this is good for the children and for me. I know exactly what I'm going to teach, giving clear guidance on what is expected and direction on how to get things done. But I rarely mention the ugly words learning objectives, success criteria and targets. The principles are there but the jargon isn't. And guess what? They still learn.

From an article in *The Guardian*, 9 August 2014

Want to silence a two-year-old? Try teaching it to ride a motorbike

I decided to introduce my son to video games. We soon found one he liked … and I mean really, really liked.

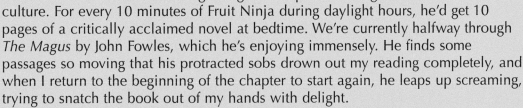

'After a while my son was shunning his regular toys in favour of "the Motorbike Game", as he calls it (it's actually called Trials Fusion).'

So I decided to introdue my two-year-old son to the world of video games. Before you accuse me of hobbling my offspring's mind, I'd like to point out that a) television is 2,000 times worse, so shove that up your Night Garden and b) I also decided to counterbalance the gaming with exposure to high culture. For every 10 minutes of Fruit Ninja during daylight hours, he'd get 10 pages of a critically acclaimed novel at bedtime. We're currently halfway through *The Magus* by John Fowles, which he's enjoying immensely. He finds some passages so moving that his protracted sobs drown out my reading completely, and when I return to the beginning of the chapter to start again, he leaps up screaming, trying to snatch the book out of my hands with delight.

Like any self-respecting 2014 toddler, he can swipe, pat and jab at games on a smartphone or tablet, but smartphone games aren't real games. They're interactive dumbshows designed to sedate suicidal commuters. And they're not just basic but insulting, often introducing themselves as free-to-play simply so they can extort money from you later in exchange for more levels or less terrible gameplay. Either that or they fund themselves with pop-up adverts that defile the screen like streaks on a toilet bowl.

I don't want him playing that horrible rubbish. I want him mainlining proper games as quickly as possible. And proper games are played with a keyboard and a mouse, or a weighty controller embellished with an intimidating array of buttons and sticks and triggers – one that melts ergonomically into any experienced gamer's hands, but makes newcomers feel like they've just picked up a Rubik's Cube designed by Salvador Dalí.

So I handed him a controller. I tried him on Super Mario World, but he didn't understand that you could move *and* jump at the same time, which limited the fun. My fun, not his. He was perfectly happy to press one button repeatedly to make Mario leap up and down on the spot. But he wouldn't time the jumps properly. He kept getting killed by the same Goomba, endlessly waddling towards him. It was excruciating to watch. So I switched the Nintendo off and tried a different console. He screamed with enthusiasm, or possibly despair. Maybe even hunger. It was getting quite late.

Eventually, after a few more missteps, I stumbled across the perfect game: Trials Fusion. It looks like an action game, but it's actually more of a physics-based puzzle. You're meant to continually adjust the stance of a motorcyclist so he doesn't fall off as he rides at speed over spectacular courses full of ramps and chasms. Despite its high difficulty level, he could make entertaining progress just by pressing the accelerator. The rider fell off all the time, but when he did he plummeted into ravines and bashed against photorealistic scenery, screaming in terror. My son found this hilarious, which is fine, OK, because it *is* hilarious. After each tumble he hurriedly tapped "retry", which is the second button he learned to locate.

Things soon escalated. One afternoon he threw a tantrum in a supermarket and I, in desperation, downloaded the iPhone version of "the Motorbike Game" (which is what he calls it), and handed it to him as he writhed screaming in the trolley seat. Bingo. Instant calm. He couldn't have been happier. Or quieter. I had to prise it from his hands later with a shoehorn, but that seemed a reasonable exchange for 30 minutes of peace.

But as with free-to-play games, the price was higher; the sting came later. Shortly afterwards, we went on holiday. He had a meltdown on the plane, so out came the Motorbike Game. Wouldn't sit still in a restaurant. Out came the Motorbike Game. Strayed perilously near the pool. Motorbike Game. It was too tempting: like having a toddler with a pause button. Inevitably, he got hooked. Hopelessly hooked.

I want the Motorbike Game. I want the Motorbike Game. That's all I heard all week, apart from him singing the theme music. Just like smoking, each individual cigarette satiated the immediate craving, while increasing his overall dependence.

Worst of all, in the iPhone version – which surprise, surprise masquerades as "free" – the bike runs out of fuel now and then, and the only way to refill the tank it is to wait for a countdown to expire (slightly harder for a two-year-old than completing a tapestry), watch an advert (evil) or to purchase in-game petrol from the App Store.

I first became aware of this when he screamed and hurled the phone across a restaurant table in a fury. I caved in immediately and, illustrating everything that's wrong with human progress, found myself spending real money on non-existent petrol for a non-existent motorbike in a desperate bid to appease an infant. Spending money to shut him up felt transgressive and undignified – but worse still, I was literally fuelling his addiction.

On our return we realised he was shunning his regular toys in favour of the Motorbike Game. There was nothing else for it. He had to go cold turkey. The Motorbike Game had to die. I deleted it from the phone and hid the Xbox controller. Neither action went down well. Having been introduced in order to avert meltdowns, the Motorbike Game was now causing them on an epic scale.

Eventually, after several days of endless and often furious requests for the Motorbike Game, he passed through the five stages of grief and came out the other side.

I walked into the kitchen where he sat calmly on the floor, playing with his wooden blocks for the first time in a week.

"That's nice," I cooed encouragingly. "What are you doing?"

"I'm playing the Motorbike Game", he replied, a little sadly.

I looked again. He was re-enacting the game. One block was the motorbike. The rest were the scenery.

It wasn't as good as the original. But it was, at least, his own.

From an article by Charlie Brooker in *The Guardian*, 11 August 2014

Types of questions: questions on both passages

The question on both passages is the only question that follows the second passage in the reading for understanding, analysis and evaluation paper. Here is an example from the SQA Higher Specimen Paper:

Both writers express their views about the importance of trees. Identify key areas on which they agree. In your answer, you should refer in detail to both passages.

You may answer this question in continuous prose or in a series of developed bullet points.

Notice that you are asked to identify the **key areas of agreement** in this question but you could also be asked to identify the key areas on which they **disagree**, or even the key areas of agreement **and** disagreement – so don't be thrown by this if it appears in your exam. The question is essentially a test of your ability to recognise what is at the heart of each passage. **It is always worth 5 marks.** When answering a question about the key areas in each passage, make sure you can identify and summarise what seem to be the main points the writer has made. Look again at the topic sentences of each paragraph – they should provide you with helpful reminders.

You can answer this question in continuous prose or in a series of developed bullet points but you might find the following 'template' helpful.

Answer

Key Area of Agreement #1: *write the first area of agreement here.*

- Evidence from passage 1: *this should be in the form of a quotation from the passage and a more generalised comment/summary by you to show your understanding of the idea presented by the writer of passage 1.*
- Evidence from passage 2: *this should be in the form of a quotation from the passage and a more generalised comment/summary by you to show your understanding of the idea presented by the writer of passage 2.*

Then **repeat** for Key Area of Agreement #2, #3 and so on.

Always try to identify at least **three** key areas in your response to this question.

Reading for Understanding, Analysis and Evaluation exam paper

Now you have had some practice with the kinds of questions asked in the Higher exam, have a go at this full length Reading for Understanding, Analysis and Evaluation paper. There are two passages and questions. Read each passage carefully and then answer the questions. Use the techniques explained earlier in the chapter and, once you have finished, check your answers against the suggested answers on pages 88–95.

Passage 1

In this passage, which is taken from an introduction to a book about evolution, the scientist Richard Dawkins describes some of the difficulties faced by those teaching the topic in schools.

TOP TIP

For extra realism, try completing past papers or practice papers 'against the clock'. Allow yourself **one hour and 30 minutes** to complete all the questions.

ONLY A THEORY

Imagine that you are a teacher of Roman history and the Latin language, anxious to impart your enthusiasm for the ancient world – for the elegiacs of Ovid and the odes of Horace, the sinewy economy of Latin grammar as exhibited in the oratory of Cicero, the strategic niceties of the Punic Wars, the generalship of Julius Caesar and the voluptuous
5   excesses of the later emperors. That's a big undertaking and it takes time, concentration, dedication. Yet you find your precious time continually preyed upon, and your class's attention distracted, by a baying pack of ignoramuses (as a Latin scholar you would know better than to say 'ignorami') who, with strong political and especially financial support, scurry about tirelessly attempting to persuade your unfortunate pupils that
10   the Romans never existed. There never was a Roman Empire. The entire world came into existence only just beyond living memory. Spanish, Italian, French, Portuguese, Catalan, Occitan, Romansh: all these languages and their constituent dialects sprang spontaneously and separately into being, and owe nothing to any predecessor such as Latin. Instead of devoting your full attention to the noble vocation of classical scholar
15   and teacher, you are forced to divert your time and energy to a rearguard defence of the proposition that the Romans existed at all: a defence against an exhibition of ignorant prejudice that would make you weep if you weren't too busy fighting it.

If my fantasy of the Latin teacher seems too wayward, here's a more realistic example. Imagine you are a teacher of more recent history, and your lessons on
20   twentieth-century Europe are boycotted, heckled or otherwise disrupted by well-organized, well-financed and politically muscular groups of Holocaust-deniers. Unlike my hypothetical Rome-deniers, Holocaust-deniers really exist. They are vocal, superficially plausible, and adept at seeming learned. They are supported by the president of at least one currently powerful state, and they include at least one bishop
25   of the Roman Catholic Church. Imagine that, as a teacher of European history, you are continually faced with belligerent demands to 'teach the controversy' and to give 'equal time' to the 'alternative theory' that the Holocaust never happened but was invented by a bunch of Zionist fabricators. Fashionably relativist intellectuals chime in to insist that there is no absolute truth: whether the Holocaust happened is a matter of personal
30   belief; all points of view are equally valid and should be equally 'respected.'

The plight of many science teachers today is not less dire. When they attempt to expound the central and guiding principle of biology; when they honestly place the living world in its historical context – which means evolution; when they explore and explain the very nature of life itself, they are harried and stymied, hassled and bullied,
35   even threatened with loss of their jobs. At the very least their time is wasted at every turn. They are likely to receive menacing letters from parents, and have to endure the sarcastic smirks and close-folded arms of brainwashed children. They are supplied with state-approved textbooks that have had the word 'evolution' systematically expunged, or bowdlerized into 'change over time'. Once, we were tempted to laugh this kind of thing
40   off as a peculiarly American phenomenon. Teachers in Britain and Europe now face the same problems.

The Archbishop of Canterbury has no problem with evolution, nor does the Pope (give or take the odd wobble over the precise palaeontological juncture when the human soul was injected), nor do educated priests and professors of theology. This is a
45   book about the positive evidence that evolution is a fact. It is not intended as an anti-religious book. I've done that, it's another T-shirt, this is not the place to wear it again. Bishops and theologians who have attended to the evidence for evolution have given up the struggle against it. Some may do so reluctantly, some enthusiastically, but all except

50 the woefully uninformed are forced to accept the fact of evolution. They may think God had a hand in starting the process off, and perhaps didn't stay his hand in guiding its future progress. They probably think God cranked the universe up in the first place, and solemnized its birth with a harmonious set of

55 laws and physical constants calculated to fulfil some inscrutable purpose in which we were eventually to play a role. But, grudgingly in some cases, happily in others, thoughtful and rational churchmen and women accept the evidence for evolution.

60 Evolution is a fact. Beyond reasonable doubt, beyond serious doubt, beyond sane, informed, intelligent doubt, beyond doubt evolution is a fact. The evidence for evolution is at least as strong as the evidence for the Holocaust, even allowing for eye witnesses to the Holocaust. It is the plain truth that we are cousins of chimpanzees, somewhat more distant cousins of monkeys, more distant cousins still of aardvarks and manatees, yet

65 more distant cousins of bananas and turnips... continue the list as long as desired. That didn't have to be true. It is not self-evidently, tautologically, obviously true, and there was a time when most people, even educated people, thought it wasn't. It didn't have to be true, but it is.

Richard Dawkins, *The Greatest Show on Earth*

Questions on passage 1

		Marks
1.	Read lines 1–6. According to the writer why is teaching Roman history and the Latin language a 'big undertaking' (line 5) and what does this require from the teacher?	4
2.	Analyse the writer's use of language in lines 6–10 to convey what he feels about the threat posed by the 'ignoramuses' (line 7).	2
3.	Referring to specific language features, how effective do you find lines 14–17 as a conclusion to the opening paragraph?	4
4.	According to the writer, what are the characteristics of the 'Holocaust-deniers' (line 21)?	2
5.	By referring to at least two features of language in lines 25–30, analyse how the writer conveys his disapproval of the situation faced by the hypothetical history teacher.	4
6.	Read lines 31–41. Analyse the writer's use of language in this paragraph to highlight his feelings of sympathy for science teachers today. You should refer in your answer to such features as word choice, sentence structure, imagery …	4
7.	Reread lines 50–59. By referring to at least one example, analyse how the writer's use of imagery reinforces his view of those who hold creationist beliefs.	2
8.	Analyse the writer's use of language in the final paragraph to emphasise his position on this subject.	3

Passage 2

The following passage is adapted from an article written by Professor Michael Reiss, Director of Education at The Royal Society, published in The Guardian.

Science lessons should tackle creationism and intelligent design. What should science teachers do when faced with students who are creationists? Definitions of creationism vary, but about 10% of people in the UK believe that the Earth is only some 10,000 years old, that it came into existence as described in the early parts of the Bible or the Qur'an
5 and that the most evolution has done is to split species into closely related species.

At the same time, the overwhelming majority of biologists consider evolution to be the central concept in biological sciences, providing a conceptual framework that unifies every aspect of the life sciences into a single coherent discipline. Equally, the overwhelming majority of scientists believe that the universe is of the order of about 13 to
10 14 billion years old.

Evolution and cosmology are understood by many to be a religious issue because they can be seen to contradict the accounts of origins of life and the universe described in the Jewish, Christian and Muslim scriptures. The issue seems like an ongoing dispute that has science and religion battling to support the credibility of their explanations.

15 I feel that creationism is best seen by science teachers not as a misconception but as a world view. The implication of this is that the most a science teacher can normally hope to achieve is to ensure that students with creationist beliefs understand the scientific position. In the short term, this scientific world view is unlikely to supplant a creationist one.

So how might one teach evolution in science lessons, say to 14 to 16-year-olds? Many
20 scientists, and some science educators, fear that consideration of creationism or intelligent design in a science classroom legitimises them.

For example, the excellent book *Science, Evolution, and Creationism* published by the US National Academy of Sciences and Institute of Medicine, asserts: 'The ideas offered by intelligent design creationists are not the products of scientific reasoning. Discussing these
25 ideas in science classes would not be appropriate given their lack of scientific support.'

I agree with the first sentence but disagree with the second. Just because something lacks scientific support doesn't seem to me a sufficient reason to omit it from a science lesson. When I was taught physics at school, and taught it extremely well in my view, what I remember finding so exciting was that we could discuss almost anything providing we
30 were prepared to defend our thinking in a way that admitted objective evidence and logical argument.

So when teaching evolution, there is much to be said for allowing students to raise any doubts they have (hardly a revolutionary idea in science teaching) and doing one's best to have a genuine discussion. The word 'genuine' doesn't mean that creationism or
35 intelligent design deserve equal time.

However, in certain classes, depending on the comfort of the teacher in dealing with such issues and the make-up of the student body, it can be appropriate to deal with the issue. If questions or issues about creationism and intelligent design arise during science lessons they can be used to illustrate a number of aspects of how science works.

40 Having said that, I don't believe that such teaching is easy. Some students get very heated; others remain silent even if they disagree profoundly with what is said.

I do believe in taking seriously and respectfully the concerns of students who do not accept the theory of evolution, while still introducing them to it. While it is unlikely

that this will help students who have a conflict between science and their religious beliefs
45 to resolve the conflict, good science teaching can help students to manage it – and to
learn more science.

Creationism can profitably be seen not as a simple misconception that careful science
teaching can correct. Rather, a student who believes in creationism has a non-scientific
way of seeing the world, and one very rarely changes one's world view as a result of a
50 50-minute lesson, however well taught.

Questions on both passages

		Marks
9.	Both writers express their views about the teaching of evolution and creationism. Identify key areas on which they disagree. In your answer, you should refer in detail to both passages.	
	You may answer this question in continuous prose or in a series of developed bullet points.	5

Critical Reading: Scottish texts – Questions

The Scottish text questions are found in Section 1 of the Critical Reading paper (the second paper in the examination).

You have to answer ONE question from

Part A, Drama

or

Part B, Prose (novels or short stories)

or

Part C, Poetry.

This part of the examination is worth **20 marks** in total and you should spend approximately **45 minutes** on it – you'll need the remaining 45 minutes to write a critical essay.

In the Scottish text questions there will be extracts printed from the drama and prose set texts. Poems will be printed in their entirety unless they are very long, in which case an extract will be printed.

Individual questions are worth **2, 3** or **4 marks**. The final question is always worth **10 marks**.

Look at the following examples of the sort of questions you can expect to be asked about the printed extract.

Drama

- *Referring to two examples of dialogue explain what this reveals about ...*
- *Choose an example of humour in this extract and explain how it is used to engage the audience's sympathy for ...*
- *By referring closely to an example of stage directions or dialogue, analyse how the tension between the two characters is made clear to the audience in lines ...*

Prose

- *Analyse how the writer makes use of word choice and sentence structure in the final paragraph of the extract to suggest ...*
- *Analyse how the writer conveys a sense of isolation in lines 15–22.*
- *By referring closely to lines 1–13, explain how the writer makes the reader aware of the narrator's attitude towards ...*

Poetry

- *By referring closely to lines 1–9, show how MacCaig's use of poetic technique creates a vivid picture of the dwarf.*
- *Evaluate the effectiveness of the final stanza as a conclusion to the poem.*
- *The main themes of the poem are introduced in the title and first stanza. Identify **one** main theme and show how poetic technique is used to introduce this theme.*

Notice that these questions often require you to **refer closely**, to **analyse** and to **evaluate the effectiveness of** …

Comment on effect

When answering these questions it is important that you do not just name a technique or identify a feature in the passage – you must also comment on its effect.

Let's look at how this works in practice. Imagine that you've been asked a question about this part of *Visiting Hour* (stanza 5) by Norman MacCaig.

Ward 7. She lies
in a white cave of forgetfulness.
A withered hand
trembles on its stalk. Eyes move
behind eyelids too heavy
to raise. Into an arm wasted
of colour a glass fang is fixed,
not guzzling but giving.
And between her and me
distance shrinks till there is none left
but the distance of pain that neither she nor I
can cross.

TOP TIP

In many ways these questions are quite similar to the sorts of questions you might be asked in the reading for understanding, analysis and evaluation paper. You can use the same approach to answer them.

Question: By referring closely to McCaig's use of poetic techniques in stanza 5, show how he conveys a sense of the patient's isolation and weakness.

In your answer you might begin by choosing to focus on the lines

'A withered hand/trembles on its stalk';

the vivid metaphor used by MacCaig to describe the patient's hand and arm.

If you then wrote any of the following as part of your answer:

1. MacCaig says 'A withered hand/trembles on its stalk'.
2. MacCaig uses a metaphor 'A withered hand trembles on its stalk' to describe the patient.
3. MacCaig uses a metaphor 'A withered hand trembles on its stalk' to describe the patient's isolation and weakness.

you would not be awarded any marks because in the first one you are merely quoting the line; in the second you simply identify the technique as a metaphor, and in the third the words of the question are just tacked on at the end.

In order to gain the marks available for the question, of course you must identify the technique – but you must also make a suitable comment on the effect(s) of that technique or feature and what it suggests to the reader.

A successful answer would look something like:

MacCaig's use of the metaphor 'A withered hand/trembles on its stalk' suggests the patient's weakness by comparing the patient's arm to a decaying plant. This makes her seem less than human. 'Withered' suggests something dried up and dying. 'Stalk' exaggerates the thinness of the arm. 'Trembles' suggests a lack of control, again highlighting the patient's weakness.

You would then also comment on:

*   'white cave of forgetfulness'
*   'eyelids too heavy/to raise'
*   'arm wasted of colour'
*   'glass fang is fixed'
*   'not guzzling but giving'
*   'the distance of pain that neither she nor I/can cross'.

The final 10-mark question will require you to analyse and comment on a feature the printed text or extract has in common with the rest of the text (if it's a novel or a play) or with other texts by the same writer.

The following pages contain three examples (drama, prose and poetry) of questions on Scottish texts.

Question on Scottish texts

Drama: *The Slab Boys*, by John Byrne

Read the extract below and then attempt the following questions. See pages 133–134 for the answers.

This extract is taken from the opening scenes of the play.

The Slab Room. Enter GEORGE 'SPANKY' FARRELL in dustcoat, drainpipe trousers, Tony Curtis hairdo, crepe-soled shoes. He crosses to his slab and starts working. Enter HECTOR MCKENZIE, similarly attired in dustcoat. He is shorter and weedier than SPANKY. He wears spectacles and carries a portable radio.

5 SPANKY: Hey ... where'd you get the wireless, Heck? Never seen you with that this morning.

HECTOR: Had it planked down the bog ... didn't want 'you-know-who' to see it.

SPANKY: Does it work? Give's a shot. (Grabs radio.) Where's Luxemburg?

HECTOR: Watch it, Spanky ... you'll break it! You can't get Luxemburg ... it's not
10 dark enough.

SPANKY: Aw – D'you need a dark wireless? I never knew that. Mebbe if we pull the aerial out a bit ... (Does so. It comes away in his hand.)

HECTOR: You swine, look what you've done!

SPANKY: Ach, that's easy fixed.

15 HECTOR: Give us it. (Twiddles knobs. Gets Terry Dene singing 'A White Sport Coat'.)

SPANKY: Good God, could you not've brung in a more modern wireless? That's donkeys out of date.

HECTOR: I like it.

20 SPANKY: That's cos you're a tube, Hector.

(Enter PHIL MCCANN in street clothes and carrying a portfolio under his arm. He sets folio down behind the door.)

Morning, Phil. You're early the day. (Consults wristwatch painted on wrist.) 'S only half eleven.

25 PHIL: Anybody been looking for us?

SPANKY: Willie Curry was in ten minutes ago looking for that lemon yellow you promised but I told him you had diarrhoea and you'd take a big dish of it down to him later on.

PHIL: (Changing into dustcoat) Who belongs to the juke box?

30 HECTOR: 'S mines.

(Enter WILLIE CURRY.)

CURRY: Ha ... there you are, McCann. Where've you been this morning? Farrell there said you were unwell.

PHIL: Er ... urn ... yes ...

35 CURRY: C'mon, what was up with you?

PHIL: Er ... touch of the ... er drawhaw.

CURRY: The what?

PHIL: Dee-oh-raw-ho ... the skitters ... it was very bad.

CURRY: Why didn't you come to me earlier? I could've got Nurse to have a look
40 at you ...

PHIL: No ... it's not what you'd cry a 'spectator sport', Mr Curly ...

CURRY: In future you report all illnesses to me ... first thing. How am I supposed to keep tabs on you lot if I don't know where the devil you are?

PHIL: I was down the lavvies ...

45 CURRY: You wouldn't get much done down there ...

PHIL: Oh, I wouldn't say that, Mr Corrie ...

CURRY: Godstruth, I don't know ... If I'd had you chaps out in Burma. Diarrhoea? There were men in my platoon fighting the Japanese with dysentery.

SPANKY: How did they fire it ... from chip baskets?

50 CURRY: Less of your damned cheek, Farrell. A couple of years in the Forces would smarten your ideas up a bit ... they'd soon have those silly duck's arse haircuts off you. And what've I told you about bringing that bloody contraption in ... eh? (Picks up radio.)

SPANKY: What contraption?

55 CURRY: How d'you expect to get any work done with that racket going on?

SPANKY: Pardon?

CURRY: Whoever owns this gadget can ask Mr Barton for it back.

(Protests from boys.)

I'll be calling back in five minutes and if you bunch are still lounging about
60 you're for the high jump, understand? Now, get on with it ... (Exit.)

PHIL: Chirpy this morning, eh?

CURRY: (Popping head round the door) Five minutes! (Exit.)

HECTOR: My bloody wireless! That was for my maw's Christmas present.

PHIL: Bless my boater, did you catch that, Cherry? A yuletide cadeau for the
65 squirt's mater and blow me if old Quelch ain't went and confiscated the blighter!

SPANKY: Christ, Nugent, that's torn it.

PHIL: Buck up, Pygmy Minimus ... Cherry and I'll think of something. Any ideas, Cherry, old chap?

SPANKY: How about a set of cufflinks?

70 PHIL: I'll wager that beast, Bunter, had a fat finger in this ...

(Enter JACK HOGG with ALAN DOWNIE.)

Yaroo! ...

SPANKY: Yeugh ...

JACK: Morning, you chaps. Just showing the new lad round the Design Room.
75 This is our last stop.

PHIL: Natch. When're you off, Jacky boy?

JACK: Alan Downie ... George Farrell ... known to the riff-raff as 'Spanky' ...

SPANKY: Watch it, Jack. Howdy, Archie ...

JACK: And this is Phil McCann ...

80 PHIL: Hi, Andy ...

JACK: And last but by all means least Hector.

HECTOR: McKenzie ... hello.

JACK: This is the Slab Room, Alan ... where the colours are ground and dished for the Designers ... you saw the patterns out there. What the lads do, basically, is dole
85 out a quantity of dry colour from those drums over there ... persian red, rose pink ...

PHIL: ... bile green ...

SPANKY: ... acne yellow ...

JACK: ... dump it on to one of these marble diff slabs ... add some gum arabic to prevent it flaking off the paper ... do we have some gum arabic? Then it's just a
90 matter of grinding ... (demonstrates). Bit of a diff from the studio, eh?

SPANKY: Why don't you vamoose, Jacky boy?

PHIL: Yeh, Plooky Chops ... them boils of yours is highly smittal.

JACK: I'm warning you, McCann.

PHIL: Keep away from me! Hector, fling us over the Dettol!

95 JACK: Jealousy will get you nowhere, McCann ... just because I'm on a desk.

SPANKY: It's a bloody operating table you want to be on, Jack. That face ... yeugh.

PHIL: You can put in for plastic surgery, you know ... on the National Health.

SPANKY: Or a 'pimplectomy'.

PHIL: It would only take about six months ...

100 SPANKY: ... and a team of surgeons ...

PHIL: ... with pliers.

JACK: (To ALAN) I've just got to dodge down the factory ... have a look at a couple of 'trials' ... shouldn't be too long. (To SPANKY and PHIL) The Boss would like you to show Alan what goes on in here ... in the way of work.
105 (To ALAN) Don't worry, you haven't been condemned to spend the rest of the day here ... I'll have a word with Bobby Sinclair, the colour consultant ... he could take you through the dyeing process ...

(SPANKY collapses into PHIL's arms.)

See you shortly ... (Exit.)

110 PHIL: Get a brush and some red paint, Heck.

HECTOR: What for?

SPANKY: To paint a cross on the door, stupid. To warn the villagers ...

HECTOR: What villagers?

PHIL: (To ALAN) OK, son, what did you say your name was again?

115 ALAN: Alan ... Alan Downie.

PHIL: Right, Eamonn ... let's show you some of the mysteries of the Slab Room. Mr Farrell ...

SPANKY: Mr Mac?

PHIL: I'm just showing young Dowdalls here some of the intricacies of our work.
120 If you and the boy would care to stand to the one side ...

SPANKY: Certainly. Hector ...

PHIL: Many thanks. Right, Alec ... this here is what we call a sink ... s-i-n-k. Now I don't expect you to pick up all these terms immediately but you'll soon get the hang of it. And this (grabs HECTOR) is what we cry a Slab Boy.

Questions

		Marks
1.	By referring closely to lines 1–16, show how the play's setting in time is established for the audience.	3
2.	By referring to two examples of dialogue in this extract, show how the playwright establishes the character of Willie Curry.	3
3.	Analyse the effect of some of the different registers of language in dialogue spoken by the characters that are evident in this extract.	4
4.	By referring to this extract and elsewhere in the play, discuss how the theme of bullying is developed in the text.	10

Total 20

Prose: *Sunset Song*, by Lewis Grassic Gibbon

Read the extract below and then attempt the following questions. See pages 135–137 for the answers.

This extract is from *Part I* (Ploughing).

So that was the college place at Duncairn, two Chrisses went there each morning, and one was right douce and studious and the other sat back and laughed a canny laugh at the antics of the teachers and minded Blawearie brae and the champ of horses and the smell of dung and her father's brown, grained
5   hands till she was sick to be home again. But she made friends with young Marget Strachan, Chae Strachan's daughter, she was slim and sweet and fair, fine to know, though she spoke about things that seemed awful at first and then weren't awful at all; and you wanted to hear more and Marget would laugh and say it was Chae that had told her. Always as Chae she spoke of him and that was an unco-like thing
10   to do of your father, but maybe it was because he was socialist and thought that Rich and Poor should be Equal. And what was the sense of believing that and then sending his daughter to educate herself and herself become one of the Rich?

But Marget cried that wasn't what Chae intended, she was to learn and be ready for the Revolution that was some day coming. And if come it never did
15   she wasn't to seek out riches anyway, she was off to be trained as a doctor, Chae said that life came out of women through tunnels of pain and if God had planned women for anything else but the bearing of children it was surely the saving of them. And Marget's eyes, that were blue and so deep they minded you of a well you peeped into, they'd grow deeper and darker and her sweet face grow so
20   solemn Chris felt solemn herself. But that would be only a minute, the next and Marget was laughing and fleering, trying to shock her, telling of men and women, what fools they were below their clothes; and how children came and how you should have them; and the things that Chae had seen in the huts of the blacks in Africa. And she told of a place where the bodies of men lay salted and white in
25   great stone vats till the doctors needed to cut them up, the bodies of paupers they were–*so take care you don't die as a pauper, Chris, for I'd hate some day if I rang a bell and they brought me up out of the vat your naked body, old and shrivelled and frosted with salt, and I looked in your dead, queer face, standing there with the scalpel held in my hand, and cried 'But this is Chris Guthrie!'*

30   That was awful, Chris felt sick and sick and stopped midway the shining path that led through the fields to Peesie's Knapp that evening in March. Clean and keen and wild and clear, the evening ploughed land's smell up in your nose and your mouth when you opened it, for Netherhill's teams had been out in that park all day, queer and lovely and dear the smell Chris noted. And something else she
35   saw, looking at Marget, sick at the thought of her dead body brought to Marget. And that thing was a vein that beat in Marget's throat, a little blue gathering where the blood beat past in slow, quiet strokes, it would never do that when one was dead and still under grass, down in the earth that smelt so fine and you'd never smell; or cased in the icy darkness of a vat, seeing never again the lowe of burning
40   whins or hearing the North Sea thunder beyond the hills, the thunder of it breaking through a morning of mist, the right things that might not last and so soon went by.

And they only were real and true, beyond them was nought you might ever attain but a weary dream and that last dark silence–Oh, only a fool loved being alive!

45 But Marget threw her arms around her when she said that, and kissed her with red, kind lips, so red they were that they looked like haws, and said there were lovely things in the world, lovely that didn't endure, and the lovelier for that. *Wait till you find yourself in the arms of your lad, in the harvest time it'll be with the stooks round about you, and he'll stop from joking–they do, you know, and that's just when their blood-pressure alters–and he'll take you like this–wait, there's not a body to see*
50 *us!–and hold you like this, with his hands held so, and kiss you like this!*

It was over in a moment, quick and shameful, fine for all that, tingling and strange and shameful by turns. Long after she parted with Marget that evening she turned and stared down at Peesie's Knapp and blushed again; and suddenly she was seeing them all at Blawearie as though they were strangers naked out of
55 the sea, she felt ill every time she looked at father and mother. But that passed in a day or so, for nothing endures.

Not a thing, though you're over-young to go thinking of that, you've your lessons and studies, the English Chris, and living and eating and sleeping that other Chris that stretches your toes for you in the dark of the night and whispers
60 a drowsy I'm you. But you might not stay from the thinking when all in a day, Marget, grown part of your life, came waving to you as you neared the Knapp with the news she was off to Aberdeen to live with an auntie there–*it's a better place for a scholar, Chae says, and I'll be trained all the sooner.*

And three days later Chae Strachan and Chris drove down to the station with
65 her, and saw her off at the platform, and she waved at them, bonny and young, Chae looked as numb as Chris felt. He gave her a lift from the station, did Chae, and on the road he spoke but once, to himself it seemed, not Chris: *Ay, Marget lass, you'll do fine, if you keep the lads at bay from kissing the bonny breast of you.*

Questions

		Marks
1.	By close reference to paragraphs 1 and 2, explain how the writer's language conveys a sense of Marget Strachan's character.	4
2.	By referring to at least two examples from paragraph 3, analyse how the writer conveys a sense of the contrast between life and death.	4
3.	By referring to two examples from paragraphs 3 and 4, analyse how the writer conveys Chris's perception of the incident with Marget.	2
4.	This extract refers to two aspects of Chris's character. By referring to this extract and from elsewhere in the novel, discuss how Grassic Gibbon conveys these aspects of Chris's character.	10
		Total 20

Poetry: 'Nil Nil' by Don Paterson

Read the extract from Don Paterson's 'Nil Nil' printed below and then attempt the following questions. See pages 137–138 for the answers.

Unknown to him, it is all that remains
of a lone fighter-pilot, who, returning at dawn
to find Leuchars was not where he'd left it,
took time out to watch the Sidlaws unsheathed
5 from their great black tarpaulin, the haar burn off Tayport
and Venus melt into Carnoustie, igniting
the shoreline; no wind, not a cloud in the sky
and no one around to admire the discretion
of his unscheduled exit: the engine plopped out
10 and would not re-engage, sending him silently
twirling away like an ash-key,
his attempt to bail out only partially successful,
yesterday having been April the 1st –
the ripcord unleashing a flurry of socks
15 like a sackful of doves rendered up to the heavens
in private irenicon. He caught up with the plane
on the ground, just at the instant the tank blew
and made nothing of him, save for his fillings,
his tackets, his lucky half-crown and his gallstone,
20 now anchored between the steel bars of a stank
that looks to be biting the bullet on this one.

In short, this is where you get off, reader;
I'll continue alone, on foot, in the failing light,
following the trail as it steadily fades
25 *into road repairs, birdsong, the weather, nirvana,*
the plot thinning down to a point so refined
  not even the angels could dance on it. Goodbye.

Questions

		Marks
1.	By referring to specific features, explain how this extract relates to the earlier parts of the poem.	3
2.	By referring closely to lines 4–16, analyse the use of poetic technique to describe the fighter pilot's experience.	4
3.	Evaluate how effective you find lines 16–21 of this extract. Your answer should deal with ideas and/or language.	3
4.	*By referring to this poem and another poem by Don Paterson you have studied discuss how he makes the reader consider the theme of time.*	**10**
		Total 20

TOP TIP

Remember that the final question in this section will **always** be worth **10** marks.

The critical essay

This part of the paper is no longer quite so daunting as it used to be in previous versions of Higher English. If you have completed a National 5 English course and sat the exam that goes with that course, then you will be familiar with the demands of writing a critical essay under timed conditions. Nevertheless there are many things you can do to improve your chances of success in this part of the examination.

The critical essay section forms the second section of the critical reading paper. It is therefore very important that you get used to writing a successful essay in around 45 minutes. There's no point in spending so much time on your chosen Scottish text question that you run out of time and can't complete your essay. The critical essay has **20 marks** allocated to it. We will look at how the essays are marked later.

The Critical Reading paper is divided into five sub sections and these will be presented in the same order each year: drama, prose, poetry, film and TV drama, and language. You have to answer any **one** question but it must be on a genre different to the one you chose in the Questions on Scottish Texts section. So if you've answered on poetry in the Questions on Scottish Texts section you cannot choose a Critical Essay question from the poetry section. You are reminded of this again in the instructions printed in the exam paper itself.

The questions are designed in such a way that they test your **knowledge and understanding** of the literary texts you have studied as part of your Higher course and your ability to **analyse and evaluate** them. The essays also test your powers of expression and must be capable of being *understood at first reading* and have *only a few errors in spelling, grammar, sentence construction, punctuation and paragraphing.*

> ## TOP TIP
>
> Remember that you *can* base your critical essay on a text printed in the Questions on Scottish Texts section as long as you stay within the requirement to answer on **two different** genres in this paper.

Let's consider each sub section of this part of the exam paper in turn.

Drama

At the start of this section is a reminder of the dramatic techniques from the play you should address in your answer. The advice for drama is as follows:

*Answers to questions on **drama** should refer to the text and to such relevant features as characterisation, key scene(s), structure, climax, theme, plot, conflict, setting ...*

There are then **three** essay questions to choose from. You should be prepared to show your knowledge of a wide range of features to be found in drama texts. The questions might make specific reference to:

- Theme
- Key scene
- Opening scene
- Concluding scene
- Central character
- Characterisation
- Relationship between characters
- Situation
- Staging/set/use of acting areas
- Dialogue
- Plot
- Structure
- Conflict
- Turning point
- Climax
- Ending
- Symbolism
- Recurring motifs
- Lighting

Prose

This section is divided into two: fiction and non-fiction. The advice for prose fiction is as follows:

*Answers to questions on **prose fiction** should refer to the text and to such relevant features as characterisation, setting, language, key incident(s), climax, turning point, plot, structure, narrative technique, theme, ideas, description ...*

There are then **three** questions on prose fiction. These are on the novel or short story. The questions might make specific reference to:

- Plot opening
- Plot ending
- Characterisation/main characters/minor characters
- Relationship between characters
- Point of view
- Setting
- Narrative method
- Narrative voice
- Structure
- Key incident or scene
- Language
- Theme

There are three questions on prose non-fiction. If you attempt one of them you are told that:

*Answers to questions on **prose non-fiction** should refer to the text and to such relevant features as ideas, use of evidence, stance, style, selection of material, narrative voice ...*

The questions might make specific reference to:

- Presentation of events in biography and autobiography
- Portrayal of society/culture/country
- Structure
- Description
- Emotional experience
- Style
- Use of humour
- Insights given by travel writing
- The writer's stance
- Persuasive language

TOP TIP

Studying as wide a range of texts as possible during your course will increase your options in the exam and enable you to write about texts you have genuinely enjoyed.

Poetry

Any essay on poetry should:

> ... *refer to the text and to such relevant features as word choice, tone, imagery, structure, content, rhythm, rhyme, theme, sound, ideas ...*

Sometimes a question will require you to write about **two** poems either by the same poet or by different poets. If you choose to answer such a question, make sure you can discuss both poems in sufficient depth.

The questions might make specific reference to:

- Theme
- Situation
- Structure
- Sound
- Rhythm and rhyme
- Form
- Imagery
- Word choice/diction
- Tone
- Closing lines
- Ambiguity
- Mood/atmosphere
- Emotion
- Poet's or speaker's stance/perspective/personality
- Location/setting
- Portrayal/exploration of a relationship
- An experience which prompts reflection on a theme
- Description/portrayal of a scene/landscape.

Film and TV drama

This section requires you to show your knowledge of media texts. **Don't** attempt a question from this section unless you have studied a media text as part of your course – however tempted you might be to 'analyse' that DVD you watched last night. Successful answers to questions from this part of the paper will:

> ... *refer to the text and to such relevant features as use of camera, key sequence, characterisation, mise en scène, editing, setting, music/sound, special effects, plot, dialogue ...*

Questions in this section require you to deal with concepts such as:

- Characterisation
- Central character
- Music
- Adaptation of novel or stage play
- Setting
- Atmosphere
- Important sequence
- Story/plot
- Subject matter
- Presentation of a theme

Language

Only a very few candidates attempt a question from this section each year. Successful answers require knowledge of a text you have studied:

> ... *and to such relevant features as register, accent, dialect, slang, jargon, vocabulary, tone, abbreviation ...*

Although the topics in this section are very interesting, they require specialist knowledge that is beyond the scope of this book.

Choosing a question

If you look at any SQA past paper or the specimen paper available on the SQA website, you will see that the questions for the Critical Essay tend to follow the same kind of pattern.

You are first asked to 'choose' a text. Remember that you *can* use a Scottish text but not the one that you used in section 1 of the paper.

Then there is a statement that will enable you to decide if the text you have studied is suitable to answer the question.

After this comes what you have to do in the essay. Often there will be two aspects to this.

Let's look at an example.

> The initial statement. If the play you have studied does not contain a conflict between two characters you will not be able to produce a relevant response.

Choose a play in which the conflict between two characters is an important feature. Briefly explain the nature of this conflict and discuss how the dramatist's presentation of this feature enhances your understanding of the play as a whole.

> The first part of this task requires you to describe the conflict. Note the word 'Briefly' – don't spend too long on this part of the essay.

> The second part of this task. This can often require a more 'sophisticated' response. An ability to 'analyse' and 'evaluate' is clearly required as you comment on the dramatist's techniques. You will also have to refer to the 'central concerns' of the play ('your understanding of the play as a whole').

Your essay must be a **relevant** response to the question. You must resist the temptation simply to write down everything you know about your chosen text. This is especially true when you are writing about poetry – you must avoid giving the examiner a 'guided tour' of the text, starting at the beginning and explaining all of the writer's techniques, even if that's how you were taught to analyse the poem in the first place. Although you do need to include enough **content** in order to provide evidence of your knowledge and understanding, analysis and evaluation, it is much better to write a shorter essay that is relevant than a longer one that does not get to grips with the question itself. Taking five minutes to plan your essay on this and then forty minutes to write it is a sensible way to allocate your time in the exam and should enable you to produce a well-constructed, thoughtful answer.

Planning a critical essay

Once you have chosen a text that will allow you to produce a relevant response and have identified the key words in the question, you should then spend some time on planning the essay.

How you do this very much depends on you. Some people like to produce a mind map or spider diagram; others prefer a list of bullet points. It doesn't matter which method you choose as long as you can do it quickly and end up with the main points you are going to make. Taking five minutes to select a question and plan your essay should mean that you don't run out of steam after twenty minutes of frantic writing followed by wondering what to say next.

Let's look at an example of this in action. Look at the following critical essay question.

> *Choose a play in which the central character is heroic yet vulnerable.*
>
> *Show how the dramatist makes you aware of both qualities and discuss how they affect your response to the character's fate in the play as a whole.*

Say you were going to use Othello as an example of a character who is 'heroic yet vulnerable', you might produce the following planning diagram to remind yourself what points you intend to make:

Here are the same ideas in a list of bullet points.

Othello

- Tragic hero
- Heroic – 'Another of his fathom they have none to lead their business'
- Vulnerable: flaws – too trusting; capacity for jealousy; lacks self-knowledge
- Outsider in Venetian society
- Believes 'honest Iago'
- Has invested everything in his love for D. 'When I love thee not …'
- Audience sympathy
- Contrast in his language (poetic style v. echoes of Iago's use of imagery)
- Key Scene: Act III Sc. 3

Once you've decided on the points you are going to make it's a good idea to **number** them so that the structure of your essay begins to take shape and you start to have an idea about how to **order** your arguments.

Writing a critical essay

Once you have a clear idea of what you are going to write, you can begin. In the potentially stress-filled environment of the examination room, it's a good idea to keep the structure of your essay as straightforward as you can.

The opening paragraph should:

- refer to the **title** of the text and its **author**
- refer to the **key words** of the question.

The main part of your essay should then develop each of the points you have decided to make. It should develop in a logical way with a clear structure. You should pay particular attention to using **topic sentences** to signpost the stages of your argument and to refer back to the **key words** of the question.

The final paragraph should:

- refer back to the key words of the question
- bring your argument to a logical conclusion.

As you write the essay remember to **express** the points you make as **effectively** as possible.

> **TOP TIP**
>
> Don't forget that it *can* sometimes be useful to think in terms of some kind of a 'formula' for your writing. You might find it helpful to think in terms of **P**oint, **E**vidence, **E**xplanation (or something similar) when constructing your paragraph. However, in the best essays such a structure shouldn't always be too obvious to the reader!

Try using the following expressions in your essay.

The author/poet/dramatist/director	
	• attempts to …
	• develops …
	• demonstrates …
	• explores …
	• conveys …
	• exploits …
	• communicates …
	• attacks …
	• satirises …
	• utilises …
	• influences …

The author/poet/dramatist/director's	
	• aim here is to …
	• intention here is to …
	• purpose here is to …

The author/poet/dramatist/director's		
	• skill	is demonstrated by …
	• artistry	
	• craft	
	• mastery	

Many critics	<ul><li>*consider that …*</li><li>*believe that …*</li><li>*have stated that …*</li><li>*have expressed the view that …*</li></ul>

It is said that …

It has often been said that …

There can be little doubt that …

This could be seen as the author's attempt at …

Try using these to link paragraphs in your essay.

<ul><li>similarly</li><li>likewise</li><li>in the same way</li></ul>	<ul><li>although</li><li>for all that</li><li>however</li><li>on the contrary</li><li>otherwise</li><li>yet</li><li>but</li><li>even so</li></ul>	<ul><li>to this end</li><li>for this reason</li><li>for this purpose</li></ul>
<ul><li>accordingly</li><li>as a consequence</li><li>as a result</li><li>hence</li><li>therefore</li><li>thus</li><li>inevitably</li></ul>	<ul><li>for example</li><li>for instance</li><li>in other words</li><li>by way of illustration</li></ul>	<ul><li>as has been noted</li><li>finally</li><li>in brief</li><li>in short</li><li>on the whole</li><li>in other words</li></ul>

How to use quotations in your critical essay

Using quotations from the novel, play, poem or film that you are writing about will enable you to provide evidence to show that you have sufficient knowledge of the text and will support your analysis and evaluation of it. But the quotations you choose to include in your essay must be relevant **and** must support your line of argument. There is no point in learning ten quotations from, say, *Othello*, and then including them in your essay if they are not relevant to the area of the text specified by the question.

It is a good idea to keep a note of useful quotations for each text you study during the course. You can do it like this:

Act, scene and line no.	Quotation	Comment
I i 65	Iago: I am not what I am.	Iago's deceitful nature is evident.
I i 88–89	Iago: … an old black ram Is tupping your white ewe.	Iago's typically coarse and bestial imagery.
I i 115–116	Iago: … your daughter and the moor are now making the beast with Two backs.	See above.
I ii 63	Brabantio: … thou hast enchanted her;	Brabantio cannot believe that his daughter would choose to marry Othello.
I iii 76–93	Othello: Most potent … … I won his daughter.	*All of this speech.* Othello's typical dignified and highly poetic style. Note that he moves into prose under the stress of emotion and degradation (IV i 35–43; 169–211).
I iii 127–169	Othello: Her father loved me … … let her witness it.	*All of this speech.* Othello's account of his courtship of Desdemona. Again, take note of the highly poetic style.
I iii 291	Brabantio: She has deceived her Father, and may thee.	Brabantio's warning to Othello. An ominous hint of what Othello will later believe.
I iii 292	Othello: My life upon her faith. Honest Iago …	Ironic, given the later events of the play. The adjective 'honest' is applied to Iago throughout the play. The audience is always aware of the irony.
I iii 395–6	Iago: … Hell and night Must bring this monstrous birth to the world's light.	Iago's plot described as a monster; something unnatural.
II i 164–173	Iago: He takes her by the palm … With As little a web as this will I Ensnare as great a fly as Cassio.	Animal imagery again. Iago as the manipulator of events and people.
II i 278–9	Iago: The Moor, howbeit that I endure him not, Is of a constant, loving, noble nature,	Even Iago recognises Othello's nobility.

| II i 285–7 | Iago: For that I do suspect the lusty Moor
Hath leaped into my seat.
The thought whereof
Doth like a poisonous mineral gnaw my inwards; | A possible motive for Iago's actions? A vivid image of what it is like to be jealous. Iago's twisted mind also suspects Cassio of sleeping with his wife (297). |

Or you can just annotate your text. Some or all of the texts you use might be available in digital versions so you could do all of this on your phone, tablet or laptop. Use *any* method that will make your revision easier.

When you are writing a critical essay in the external exam at Higher, it's just you, a pen, a piece of paper and what's inside your head. So you must learn the quotations to use by heart. It's a good idea to keep them short – the exam isn't really a memory test, even although it can feel a bit like that sometimes!

If the quotation is a short one (a single word or short phrase), you can simply include it in the sentence you are writing (remembering to put it inside inverted commas).

For example:

Othello's continual reference to his old comrade as 'honest Iago' is a good example of Shakespeare's use of irony in the play.

or

Brabantio believes Othello has 'enchanted' Desdemona.

or

In the expression, 'the engine plopped out' Paterson uses onomatopoeia to almost comic effect.

TOP TIP

Beware the dangers of 'micro-analysis' when writing about longer prose and drama texts. Questions about these usually require you to deal with the 'big issues' of characterisation, theme, setting, etc. and that is what you should concentrate on. Don't waste time, for example, discussing the significance of individual words in a particular sentence – your marker will not be impressed!

If the quotation is a longer one (a whole line or more from the text), you can do one of the following:

Add it to the end of your sentence.

When confronted with what seems an ugly situation Othello commands everyone to 'Keep up your bright swords, for the dew will rust them'.

or

Place it, sandwiched, between the two parts of your sentence.

Othello's command

'Keep up your bright swords, for the dew will rust them'

shows his ability to defuse a potentially ugly situation.

Introduce the quotation with a verb of saying and a colon or comma.

As MacCaig tells us,

'She lies

in a white cave of forgetfulness.'

or

Neil states,

'Yonder's a room with fifty rooms ... every one of them three times the size of our hut, and nearly all of them empty.'

Longer quotations like the above should be placed on a new line for the sake of clarity in your essay.

You will also see some writers simply using a colon to introduce a quotation.

For example:

Tulloch quickly takes the side of the cone-gatherers:

'I have questioned them my lady ... and I saw what happened; and I find no fault in them.'

or

MacCaig is determined not to give in to his feelings:

'I will not feel, I will not

feel, until

I have to.'

The danger with this last method is that it can make your essay seem rather staccato and disjointed as the essay becomes simply one point after another, each followed by a quotation. You will find it difficult to construct any kind of fully developed, focused argument if you rely too much on this method.

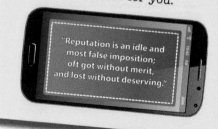

TOP TIP

To help you memorise your quotations, write them on sticky post-it notes and put them around your house in the run up to the exam. Fridge door; bathroom cabinet; bedside table – it doesn't matter where as long as they help jog your memory. You could enter and save them on your phone – as long as you remember **not** to take it with you into the exam! There are numerous free 'flash card' apps available that you could use. Search for 'flash cards' in the app store and see which ones work best for you.

"Reputation is an idle and most false imposition; oft got without merit, and lost without deserving."

Example critical essays

Finally, let's look at how all of this is put together, from reading the question to the finished essay.

> *Choose a **novel** in which one character generates hostility from one or more than one other character.*
>
> *Explain the nature of the hostility and go on to discuss how the novelist's use of it adds to your understanding of the novel as a whole.*

Example 1

We'll be using Robin Jenkins' novel *The Cone-Gatherers*, as it is an appropriate text to use but you could use **any** novel you have studied **provided it matches the description in the first part of the question** (see the words highlighted in blue).

The key words of the question have been highlighted. Here's an example of the sort of notes you could produce to remind you of what to write.

First part of question:
- Calum generates hostility from Duror (+ Lady Runcie Campbell).
- Description of Calum.
- Why Duror hates him.
  - Personification of all that's wrong in his life.
  - Defiled his 'sanctuary'.
  - Revolted by anything misshapen or deformed.
  - Descent into madness.
  - Deer drive (LRC's hostility toward Calum).
  - Accusations against Calum.
  - End of novel – death of Calum.

Second part of question:
- Theme of good v. evil.
- Calum represents good and is sacrificed at the end.
- Closing lines– LRC's moment of catharsis.
- Jenkins' ending leaves the reader (like LRC) with hope.

With these (brief) notes in front of you, you could then write something like this in the remaining forty minutes or so you will have left.

TOP TIP

You should **always** take time to plan your essay – don't be put off by other people frantically scribbling as soon as the invigilator tells you to start.

Opening paragraph identifies text and author and refers back to the question.

In 'The Cone-Gatherers' by Robin Jenkins we see the character Calum generate hostility from the evil gamekeeper Duror.

Jenkins makes the reader sympathise with Calum, a hunchback who is gathering cones with his brother in the woods of the Runcie-Campbell estate during the Second World War. Although he is deformed Jenkins portrays him as 'honest, generous and truly <u>meek</u>' and someone who is close to the world of nature. He is an expert climber and is 'as indigenous as squirrel or bird' in the trees on the estate. Jenkins effectively develops the character as someone who does not understand why there should be suffering in the world and throughout the novel he is portrayed as a 'Christ-like' figure.

> Quotations used to show knowledge of the text and to support the points made in the essay.

> Topic sentence

Calum generates hostility from Duror for many reasons. Duror 'hated and despised' the cone-gatherers and feels that they have defiled the wood which 'had always been his stronghold and sanctuary'. Through skilful characterisation, Jenkins portrays Duror's suffering. His wife has become hugely obese, their relationship has broken down and his attempts to sign up to fight in the war have been refused. Calum represents everything that is wrong in Duror's life. Jenkins tells us

'For many years his life had been stunted, misshapen, obscene and hideous; and this misbegotten creature was its personification.'

In addition to this Duror has always been revolted by anything misshapen or deformed and Jenkins even suggests that he sympathises with Hitler's treatment of 'idiots and cripples'. Duror is portrayed by Jenkins as a man descending into madness. He uses the image of a tree 'still showing green leaves' but with death 'creeping along the roots' to describe Duror and the reader is always aware of Duror's true nature and also that he is 'alone in his obsession'.

Duror uses Calum's unwilling involvement in the deer drive to try and remove him from the wood. Ironically it is at the deer drive that Duror's madness first shows in public when he kills the deer, confusing it with his wife Peggy. Calum attempts to save the deer but now also generates hostility from Lady Runcie Campbell who is annoyed that the event has become 'a shocking and demeaning spectacle'. Tulloch, a very 'moral' character, speaks up for the cone-gatherers. However, Duror's twisted mind also leads him to accuse Calum of exposing himself in the wood.

In the tense final chapter of the novel, the hostility Duror feels toward Calum leads to the killing of Calum and his own suicide.

> Now the essay begins to deal with the second part of the question.

Thus, Robin Jenkins uses this hostility to explore the theme of good versus evil and so adds to the reader's understanding of the novel as a whole. Calum's child-like goodness (a quality which he shares with Roderick) and his pity and concern for the animals of the wood make the reader sympathise with him. His 'sacrifice' at the end of the novel cleanses the wood of evil and gives hope for the future. Jenkins again suggests a similarity to Jesus' death on the Cross as 'he hung in a twisted fashion' in the tree after Duror shoots him. The cones and blood which fall from him are another suggestion of this religious symbol.

After the two deaths (and Roderick's return to safety), Lady Runcie-Campbell undergoes a moment of catharsis and as she cries 'pity, and purified hope, and joy, welled up in her heart.' The reader experiences this too as we read this very powerful and thought-provoking climax to the novel.

Jenkins' ending leaves the reader (like Lady Runcie-Campbell) with hope. Although he allows the hostility between Calum and Duror to culminate in their deaths, evil is defeated even if at great human cost. As a result, the reader is left with a greater understanding of the theme of good versus evil and of the novel as a whole.

> Concluding paragraph refers back to the key words of the question.

This essay is 623 words long. You should be able to write something of similar length in the time available to you in the exam.

Example 2

Here is another example of a critical essay. Read it carefully to see how the writer has constructed a relevant response to the question.

> *Choose a poem which you find emotionally unsettling or intellectually challenging.*
>
> *Show how the poem elicits the response from you and discuss how it contributes to your understanding of the central concerns of the poem.*

Donald Paterson's 'Nil Nil' is a poem the reader finds intellectually challenging. The poem presents you with what seems at first to be two separate 'stories' using a mixture of vivid and sometimes bizarre images. These stories are in fact linked and the reader is left to consider the connections between them and also the connections between them and the epigraph and the epilogue. Paterson skilfully challenges the reader to consider the central concerns of the poem: nothingness and loss.

The structure of the poem presents the reader with the first intellectual challenge as we are made to think about how the four separate sections are connected. The epigraph says it is a search for meaning but as it is attributed to the fictional literary theorist, Francois Aussemain, who appears in other Don Paterson poems, the reader is immediately suspicious. Paterson links ideas and images throughout the poem and the reader is challenged to find these patterns. In the epigraph we are told about 'abandoned histories' which 'plunge on into deeper and deeper obscurity' and we then see that these ideas are picked up in the two 'stories' of the poem: the decline of the football club and the death of the airman whose fuel tank 'blew/and made nothing of him'. Paterson's use of a vivid image in the epigraph 'the vast rustling map of Burgundy ... settling over it like a freshly starched sheet' is echoed in the second 'story' when the fighter-pilot sees 'the Sidlaws unsheathed/from their great black tarpaulin'. The epilogue addresses the reader directly 'In short, this is where you get off ...' and continues the idea of things reducing to nothingness with its references to 'failing light'; 'nirvana' and 'the plot thinning down'. This is a poem aware of itself as fiction and so we are challenged to make sense of what it really means.

Paterson also challenges the reader intellectually in his account of the long decline of the football club in the first 'story' as we are forced to consider the significance of ' ... the fifty year slide into Sunday League'. This section of the poem begins with a description of an old film of the club's greatest success, emphasised by Paterson's word choice: 'From the top' and 'zenith'. The long description of decline which follows includes interesting juxtapositions ('long hoick forward' and 'balletic') and vivid images:

> ' ... a shaky pan to the Erskine St End
>
> where a plague of grey bonnets falls out of the clouds'

Paterson's use of the word 'plague', with its connotations of disease and decay, is particularly effective here at signalling the imminent decline of the club. There is humour too, in the descriptions of

> '... grim fathers and perverts with Old English Sheepdogs
>
> lining the touch, moaning softly.'

and

> ' ... two little boys — Alastair Watt, —
>
> who answers to "Forty", and wee Horace Madden,
>
> so smelly the air seems to quiver above him'

This use of black humour and cartoon-like images stops the poem from becoming merely sentimental or overtly nostalgic — it forces us to reconsider Paterson's presentation of the central concerns of loss and nothingness.

References to loss and nothingness appear throughout this section of the poem: 'detaching like bubbles'; 'dwindling half-hearted kickabouts' and these are reinforced by Paterson's use of listing

> ' ... the stopped swings, the dead shanty-town
>
> of allotments, the black shell of Skelly dry cleaners'.

Paterson even makes Horace live in a 'cul-de-sac' — a road to nowhere.

The use of the 'stone' as the hinge between the two 'stories' is particularly effective. It is a grim reminder of all that remains of the 'lone fighter-pilot' but his is also an 'abandoned history' — his story is 'Unknown' to Horace. In this section of the poem, Paterson continues to challenge the reader to find meaning in all the negatives he uses:

> '... no wind, not a cloud in the sky
>
> and no one around'

and

> '... sending him silently
>
> twirling away like an ash-key'

But these more serious images are also undercut by Paterson's wit and humour. The bizarre image of the airman pulling his ripcord and

> ' ... unleashing a flurry of socks
>
> like a sackful of doves rendered up to the heavens
>
> in private irenicon.'

makes the reader try and reconcile the cartoon-like description and the formality of the word 'irenicon' — a 'proposal designed to promote peace'.

The fighter-pilot's ignominious end — 'made nothing of him, save for his fillings, / his tackets, his lucky half-crown and his gallstone' — is a stark reminder that we are all reduced to nothing at the end of our lives. The poem's title, 'Nil Nil', then seems so much more than just a reference to a football score.

In conclusion, it is clear that Don Paterson's 'Nil Nil' is a poem which challenges the reader intellectually. Through its effective use of structure and imagery, its mix of the serious and the comic, and its awareness of itself as a poem, the reader is forced to question how we interpret our 'histories' and to consider the 'dull and terrible facts' of loss and our decline into nothingness.

Preparing for the exam

It's likely you will study at least three genres during your Higher English course. Consequently you would be well advised to prepare at least one text from all three prior to the exam. Even though you will only write an essay about one of them, you need the others as an 'insurance policy' should the questions in one of your preferred sections not quite 'fit' your choice of text. It is important to revise and prepare a number of different aspects of each text (use of setting, characterisation, narrative style, theme). You will also increase your chances of success by studying as wide a range of texts as time allows during your course. That way you will be able to write

about something you have genuinely enjoyed reading or watching. The 'minimalist' approach of only studying your chosen Scottish text(s) and only one other text in a different genre and then practising essay after essay on them is unlikely to give you much of an insight into the study of literature. During your course you should, depending on the resources available in your school, be able to cover say a novel, one or two short stories and/or some shorter pieces of prose fiction; a play or a film and a selection of poetry – although the number and variety of texts taught will be different from school to school.

You must revisit and revise your texts throughout your course. Just because you finish looking at a novel in class in October, don't then leave it on the shelf until just before the exam. You must take responsibility for your own learning and keep updating your notes and knowledge throughout the year.

TOP TIP

It's a good idea to buy cheap copies of your longer texts for yourself – you'll easily find older second hand editions on sites such as Amazon and Abebooks – so you can annotate them in any ways that will make your revision easier.

Look carefully at the feedback you get from your teacher on any practice essays that you do (especially those in a prelim) and try to avoid making the same mistakes in your next essays; but on no account should you learn an essay off by heart in the hope of using it in the exam – even if you got a good mark for it. The critical essay paper rewards your ability to think on the day of the exam and it is highly unlikely that you will find a question that corresponds exactly with one you have done earlier in your course. Your teacher will probably show you 'exemplar' essays as you prepare for the exam. They are to show you the principles of effective essay writing (structure, topic sentences, links between sections, use of evidence and quotation) but they are not designed to be memorised and reproduced on the day of the exam itself. The key thing to remember is to have enough things to say about the texts you have studied and then *select* from that body of knowledge in order to write a relevant response to the exam question.

How the critical essay is marked

All critical essays are marked on a scale of 0–20. The table below shows what markers are looking for in an essay that is just good enough to pass (12–10 marks) and what they are looking for in an essay that gets the best marks (20–19).

	Marks 20–19	Marks 12–10
Knowledge and understanding The critical essay demonstrates:	• a thorough knowledge and understanding of the text • a perceptive selection of textual evidence to support a line of argument which is fluently structured and expressed • a perceptive focus on the demands of the question	• an adequate knowledge and understanding of the text • adequate textual evidence to support a line of thought which is adequately structured and expressed • an adequate focus on the demands of the question
Analysis The critical essay demonstrates:	• a perceptive analysis of the effect of features of language/filmic techniques	• an adequate analysis of the effect of features of language/filmic techniques
Evaluation The critical essay demonstrates:	• a committed, evaluative stance with respect to the text and the task	• adequate evidence of an evaluative stance with respect to the text and the task
Technical accuracy The critical essay demonstrates:	• few errors in spelling, grammar, sentence construction, punctuation and paragraphing • the ability to be understood at first reading	

The language of the marking instructions can sometimes seem not particularly 'user-friendly' so let's think about what some aspects of these criteria actually mean.

• Demonstrating 'thorough knowledge and understanding' of the text just means you need to show that you know more than just what happens in a novel or short story or poem. You need to show understanding of the **themes or ideas** the writer explores in the text. For example, you would need to show that you understand that the play *Othello* is not just about a general who is tricked into believing his wife is unfaithful and who then kills her and then himself, but that Shakespeare is using the play to explore the corrosive effects of jealousy and the very nature of evil itself. In an essay on *Sunset Song* you would need to show that you understand not just the major events in Chris Guthrie's life but also that the novel deals with the end of a way of life for a particular section of Scottish society. An essay on Norman MacCaig's *Visiting Hour* won't just give details about the speaker in the poem's visit to a hospital; it will also refer to MacCaig's musings on confronting our mortality.

- Demonstrating an 'analysis of the effect of features of language/filmic technique' requires you to explain the various **techniques** used by the writer or director (remember that you are given a reminder of the sort of things to mention in the boxes at the start of each section of the question paper). These explanations must be used to provide evidence for the line of argument that you adopt in response to the question.

- If you choose to write about texts you have **genuinely enjoyed and/or found interesting**, then it will be easier for you to demonstrate 'a committed, evaluative stance with respect to the text and task' and say something about its effectiveness. Don't go 'over the top' in what you say about a text or writer in an attempt to illustrate this! It always sounds artificial when candidates write things like '*Larkin's brilliant use of alliteration helps the reader to realise this*' or '*Jenkins' superb characterisation brings Calum to life.*'

- The requirement for technical accuracy recognises that you are writing in the stressful setting of the exam room with no opportunity to draft and redraft your essay. Nevertheless you must do all you can to avoid common (and, at this level, very basic) mistakes such as:

  ➢ Comma splice – where you join ('splice') sentences together with commas rather than ending a sentence with a full stop and then starting a new one.

  ➢ Inconsistent spelling of common words – if you know you've got problems in this area make a word list as you go through the course and make learning these spellings a part of your revision routine.

  ➢ Using slang ('*Shakespeare uses well effective imagery …*'), colloquial language ('*Othello thinks Desdemona is cheating on him …*'), 'text-speak' ('*The problem 4 Othello is …*'), abbreviations and symbols ('*Othello & Iago …*').

  ➢ Failure to organise your essay into paragraphs – the planning you do prior to starting the essay will give you a ready-made paragraph plan.

  ➢ Incorrect use of apostrophes.

  ➢ Writing expressions such as '*a lot*' as one word.

Once the marker has read the essay thoroughly he or she will then give it a mark according to the following scale (this time shown in full).

	Marks 20–19	Marks 18–16	Marks 15–13	Marks 12–10	Marks 9–6	Marks 5–0
Knowledge and understanding The critical essay demonstrates:	• a thorough knowledge and understanding of the text • a perceptive selection of textual evidence to support your line of argument which is fluently structured and expressed • perceptive focus on the demands of the question	• a secure knowledge and understanding of the text • use of detailed textual evidence to support your line of thought which is coherently structured and expressed • a secure focus on the demands of the question	• a clear knowledge and understanding of the text • use of clear textual evidence to support your line of thought which is clearly structured and expressed • clear focus on the demands of the question	• an adequate knowledge and understanding of the text • adequate textual evidence to support your line of thought which is adequately structured and expressed • adequate focus on the demands of the question	• limited evidence of knowledge and understanding of the text • limited textual evidence to support your line of thought which is structured and expressed in a limited way • limited focus on the demands of the question	• very little knowledge and understanding of the text • very little textual evidence to support your line of thought which shows very little structure or clarity of expression • very little focus on the demands of the question
Analysis The critical essay demonstrates:	• a perceptive analysis of the effect of features of language/filmic techniques	• a detailed analysis of the effect of features of language/filmic techniques	• clear analysis of the effect of features of language/filmic techniques	• adequate analysis of the effect of features of language/filmic techniques	• limited analysis of the effect of features of language/filmic techniques	• very little analysis of features of language/filmic techniques
Evaluation The critical essay demonstrates:	• a committed, evaluative stance with respect to the text and the task	• an engaged evaluative stance with respect to the text and the task	• a clear evaluative stance with respect to the text and the task	• adequate evidence of an evaluative stance with respect to the text and the task	• limited evidence of an evaluative stance with respect to the text and the task	• very little evidence of an evaluative stance with respect to the text and the task
Technical accuracy The critical essay demonstrates:	• few errors in spelling, grammar, sentence construction, punctuation and paragraphing • the ability to be understood at first reading		• adequate spelling, grammar, sentence construction, punctuation and paragraphing		• significant errors in spelling, grammar, sentence construction, punctuation and paragraphing which impedes understanding	

Which mark your essay is awarded in the category is down to how confidently the marker can place the essay in that category.

Some further advice

Short stories

Don't think that just because a short story is not as long as a novel it will be an easier text to study and write about in the exam. A well-crafted short story will make effective use of techniques specific to this genre and this can make it challenging to write about. Remember that you might be required to write about **two** short stories.

Non-fiction

If you want to prepare for a question from this part of the prose section you need to study texts such as essays (very different from *your* critical essays), travel writing, biography and autobiography, works on current affairs and politics, philosophy, etc. Remember that the techniques used by the writer in these kind of texts are **different** from those used in prose fiction. You should look at the techniques mentioned in the prose non-fiction advice above as a starting point for your studies.

Poetry

The danger of the 'guided tour' has already been mentioned. You must avoid providing a line-by-line analysis of the poem. If your essay is no more than a series of quotations followed by comments it will not 'address the central concerns of the text' and will not pass. Although it is true you cannot offer an analysis of a poem without quoting from the text you must make sure these quotations are being used by you to provide evidence to support the line of argument in your essay.

Film and TV drama

Questions from this section should be dealt with just like those in the drama, prose and poetry sections. You will need to be confident that you can make effective use of the appropriate technical terms (*mise en scène*, camera angles, sound, costume, ideology, lighting, etc.) to support you argument.

Practice critical essay questions

Try these against the clock (give yourself 45 minutes).

Drama

1. Choose a play which made you reconsider your attitude to an important issue.

   Show how the dramatist introduces this issue and go on to discuss the effectiveness of the dramatic techniques employed to make you consider the issue in a new light.

2. Choose a play in which aspects of staging (lighting, music, set, stage directions …) seem particularly important.

   Discuss how effective you find the use of these in the dramatist's exploration of the central concerns of the play.

3. Choose a play in which a central character is faced with a difficult choice.

   Briefly give an outline of the circumstances which lead up to this situation and go on to discuss how the dramatist makes you aware of the consequences of the character's decision.

Prose fiction

4. Choose a **novel or short story** in which the style of writing greatly impressed you.

   Show how the writer's chosen style added to your understanding and appreciation of the central concerns of the text.

5. Choose a **novel** set in a location which is unfamiliar to you.

   Briefly describe the setting and go on to show how, despite the unfamiliarity, the novelist is able to make you consider themes which are universal.

6. Choose a **novel or short story** in which there is conflict between two characters.

   Briefly outline the nature of the conflict and go on to show how the writer uses it to develop a central concern of the text.

Prose non-fiction

7. Choose a **non-fiction text** which seems to reveal a lot about the writer's point of view on a particular topic.

   Briefly describe what this point of view seems to be and go on to discuss in detail how this is revealed through his or her writing.

8. Choose a piece of **travel writing** in which the writer's use of language gave you a new perspective on somewhere you were already familiar with.

   Describe how the writer uses language to give you this new perspective.

9. Choose a piece of **biography** or **autobiography** which includes an account of a shocking experience.

   Briefly describe the experience and then discuss how the writer conveys the shocking nature of it.

Poetry

10. Choose two poems which seem to have similar central concerns.

    Explain what the central concerns of both poems are and go on to discuss which poem you feel deals more effectively with them.

11. Choose a poem which you feel says something important to today's society.

    Discuss how effectively the poet's techniques help to convey this message.

12. Choose a poem in which you feel the content is enhanced by the poet's choice of a particular poetic form.

    Explain in detail how the choice of form adds to your understanding of the central concerns of the text.

Film and TV drama

13. Choose a **film** or **TV drama** in which a character seems isolated from the rest of society.

    Discuss how effective you find the film or programme makers' representation of this character and go on to explain how this adds to your appreciation of the text as a whole.

14. Choose a film or television drama which subverts the conventions of its own genre.

    Explain how the film or programme makers' subversion of the genre enhances your appreciation of the text as a whole.

15. Choose a film or television programme in which the opening sequence is particularly effective in introducing the central concerns of the text.

    Explain how this effective introduction to the central concerns was achieved by the film or programme makers.

How is your writing portfolio assessed?

Let's start with a reminder of the ways by which your writing is assessed as part of your Higher English course. As part of the course assessment you have to send a Writing Portfolio to SQA. The portfolio consists of two writing pieces: one creative piece and one discursive piece.

The creative writing piece could be:

- a personal essay (an account of a personal experience and its effects on you)

  or

- a reflective essay (a bit more sophisticated than the personal essay – you could reflect on an idea; an experience; a concept or issue)

  or

- an imaginative piece (short story, drama script, poem, episode from a novel).

The discursive writing piece could be:

- an argumentative essay (exploring two or more points of view with a line of argument clearly emerging)

- a persuasive essay (in which you try to convince the reader to agree with you on a particular subject)

- a report (using information from at least two sources).

Let's consider the unit assessment in more detail. Each piece of writing you produce must be **no more than 1300** words long. **Each piece is marked out of 15**. The combined score out of **30** is added to your marks from the external exam to determine your final grade.

The following marking tables show you the differences between writing that is just good enough to pass (7–9 marks) and very good writing (13–15 marks).

Creative writing piece		
	15–13 marks	**9–7 marks**
Content	<ul><li>Committed attention to purpose and audience.</li><li>Strong creative qualities.</li><li>Evident command of the genre.</li><li>Thematic concerns that are clearly introduced and developed.</li><li>Ideas/feelings/experiences which are explored with a strong degree of mature reflection/self-awareness/involvement/insight/sensitivity.</li><li>The writer's personality and individuality.</li></ul>	<ul><li>Adequate attention to purpose and audience.</li><li>Adequate creative qualities.</li><li>Understanding of the genre.</li><li>Thematic concerns which are introduced.</li><li>Ideas/feelings/ experiences which are explored with an adequate sense of reflection and involvement.</li><li>The writer's personality.</li></ul>

Creative writing piece		
	15–13 marks	**9–7 marks**
Style	• Linguistic features of the chosen genre used skilfully to create a strong impact. • Confident and varied expression. • An effective structure, which enhances the purpose/meaning.	• Linguistic features of the chosen genre used successfully. • Adequate expression. • An adequate structure.

Discursive writing piece		
	15–13 marks	**9–7 marks**
Content	• Committed attention to purpose and audience. • Full understanding and engagement. • Evidence of full research and selection, as appropriate. • A clear and sustained line of thought/convincing stance.	• Adequate attention to purpose and audience. • Adequate understanding. • Evidence of relevant research and selection, as appropriate. • A line of thought/clear stance.
Style	• Linguistic features of the chosen genre used comprehensively to argue/discuss/persuade and convey depth and complexity of thought/objectivity/insight/persuasive force. • Confident and varied expression. • An effective structure, which enhances the purpose/meaning.	• Linguistic features of the chosen genre used adequately to argue/discuss/persuade and convey thought/objectivity/insight/persuasive force. • Adequate expression. • An adequate structure.

Your Writing Portfolio must be submitted on the SQA approved template. Your teacher/lecturer will tell you more about this requirement. You can access further information and download the template from the 'Submitting Coursework' section of the SQA Higher English web page available at http://www.sqa.org.uk/sqa/47904.html

Producing pieces of writing for your portfolio

If you have done National 5 or Intermediate 2 English you will already have experience of producing pieces of writing in a number of different forms and genres so Higher English is about **refining and developing** the skills you already possess.

Since the requirement is no more detailed than for you to produce **one** broadly creative and **one** broadly discursive piece you obviously have a wide range of subjects to choose from. For example you could write:

- A short story set on a Dundee housing estate.
- An opening chapter of novel about a girl's fraught relationship with her mother.
- A sonnet about the passing of time.
- A drama script involving three characters on a Glasgow bus.
- A piece that explores the arguments for and against creating more wind farms in Scotland.
- A piece that attempts to persuade the reader that schools are outdated institutions.
- A piece in which you reflect on your experience of what it means to be a young adult living in Scotland today.
- A report on the benefits and drawbacks of Edinburgh's new tram system.

These are just examples and there are more suggestions later in this chapter.

Planning your writing

It doesn't matter **which** kind of writing you choose to do (although you are well advised to attempt something at which you are already reasonably competent), what is important is that the writing is **your** work. Your teacher should ask you for the following at each stage of the writing process in order to guarantee the authenticity of what you produce:

* A draft title and proposal.
* An outline plan.
* A first draft.
* A final version.

A draft title, proposal and outline plan for a persuasive piece of writing might look something like this:

Date:	Pupil name:	Language study unit – writing
Proposed title: *Education 2.0 – Why our schools are failing to pass the test*		Genre: persuasive

Proposal

In this essay I am going to persuade the reader to agree with my point of view that schools are no longer fit for purpose and do not provide their pupils with an education experience that is relevant to the needs of society in the twenty-first century. I will show that they are institutions that have remained largely unchanged since the early years of the last century and that our insistence on gathering large groups of young people together in huge buildings and then dividing them into groups based on arbitrary principles, rules and flawed statistics is no longer an effective way of educating young people today. I will also look at how information technology is radically altering how we learn and how we interact with others and that this means we need a complete overhaul of what we want our schools to do.

Teacher's initials:

Date:

Outline

Introduction:

- Description of typical school day from thirty years ago (classes, timetables, buildings, bells etc. etc.) – shows how little pupils' experience has changed – contrast with radical changes in society and technology – suggest schools need to change.

Points I intend to make:

- Maintaining school buildings is a huge drain on the public purse (use local authority statistics).
- Very few of us will ever work in such large 'communities' again – why corral young people into these buildings? Once we leave school most people now work in small teams and more than ever are working from home.
- Acknowledge the counter argument about the 'socialising' effect of schools but dismiss this with reference to the negative aspects of school life such as bullying.
- Examples of successful learning outwith school.
- Point out how information technology is embedded within our lives – ref. to internet, social networking – how this has changed the way we interact with others.
- Point out how information technology has changed the way we learn – Wikipedia etc. – schools' own greater use of websites, virtual learning environments, GLOW – so why the need for 'traditional' classrooms?
- Health risks – easy for viruses such as flu to spread in large schools etc.

Conclusion

- Reiterate points made and end with strong closing statement.

Teacher's initials:

Date:

The first draft

Once your teacher has had a look at your proposals you can start work on a first draft. Remember that a word-processed draft will be easier for you to edit and amend before you produce the final version.

Let's see what the introductory paragraphs of our persuasive piece might look like. Remember to make use of the language techniques you have come across in your study of close reading passages.

Starts with a command – involves the reader	*Education 2.0 – Why our schools are failing to pass the test*
	First draft

Suggests 'restriction'

Picture the scene. The dutiful pupil dressed in full school uniform arrives at her local secondary school. It is a large concrete and glass box; a box she shares with 1000 other dutiful souls. Her day is mapped out before her; a day delineated by the grid squares of her timetable. A bell rings and she dutifully makes her way to her registration room. Another bell rings and she dutifully carries her bag full of jotters and folders to her first class. Her teacher hands out the textbooks and the pupil dutifully begins to work through the examples ...

This dutiful pupil is receiving her education in a Scottish secondary school in 2011, but the year could have been 2001, 1991, 1981 or 1971. Outwith school, however, things are very different for this pupil compared with her sisters of forty, thirty, twenty or even ten years ago. In school, she is hemmed in; at home she can roam the digital world at will. This same dutiful pupil goes home to watch her favourite TV shows online, updates her Facebook profile and chats to friends and relatives in Germany and Australia. She then sharpens up her guitar playing with a quick tutorial from a useful website and ends her day by making another entry on her blog. How can imprisoning her in a concrete and glass box for six years possibly be to the benefit of this young person?

Repetition of 'dutiful'/ 'dutifully' suggests someone meekly following instructions

Word choice suggests unflattering image of school building

Connotations of lack of freedom

List of dates suggests unchanging nature of school experience over time

Balanced sentence around a semi-colon 'hinge'

Paragraph ends with a thought-provoking question

Emotive language to elicit sympathy from the reader

Chapter 6: The writing portfolio

Once a first draft has been completed, you should ensure it contains the features required for an effective piece of writing at this level. Here is a checklist for persuasive writing:

Discursive: persuasive	
Strong opening statement	
Clear structure	
Effective use of linkage between sections/arguments	
Emotive vocabulary	
Arguments supported by evidence (statistics etc.) where appropriate	
Acknowledgement and rejection of any counter-arguments	
Direct address to the reader	
Repetition	
Climax	
Contrast	
Contrast within a list	
Use of analogy and/or illustration	
Repetition	
Listing for effect (especially in groups of three)	
Effective use of imagery	
Gives a clear sense that the writer is *convinced* of their case	
Effective use of 'attitude markers': *Surely, ... Clearly, ... Happily, ...*	
Strong closing statement	
Sources consulted are clearly stated	

Once you have completed a first draft of your writing your teacher will be able to give you feedback. This feedback will usually be in the form of suggesting improvements you might make to your piece. You might be asked to look again at the way you have structured your writing (perhaps you need to reorder your ideas) or you might be told that your punctuation and spelling are not yet accurate enough. Your teacher is **not**, however, allowed to indicate specific, individual errors for you to go away and correct. Proofreading and editing of your work are **your** responsibility.

Features and techniques of each genre

If you have decided what kind of writing you want to do, here's a reminder of the features and techniques to use. We've already looked at those required for persuasive writing so let's consider a short story (creative/imaginative), a reflective piece (creative/imaginative), an argumentative piece (discursive) and a drama script (creative/imaginative). There's an exemplar opening with comments and a checklist for each genre for you to refer to. You could try continuing each piece for practice. Remember to make use of the appropriate techniques.

The Hunted

(short story)

First draft

Story starts 'in medias res' – in the middle of the action

She turned the key. Nothing. She turned the key again. Still nothing. A small bubble of fear tried to rise in her chest. She willed herself to ignore it and turned the key again. This time the engine coughed and caught. She felt the small bubble burst and she pressed her foot down on the accelerator.

Minor sentence helps create a tense atmosphere

Personification suggests hostility and amplifies the mood of tension

She hated driving on her own through this part of the city. She hated the empty streets; the feeling that people had given up on it. Ugly houses leered at her from either side. *Everything's fine. This is something you can do. It's not going to happen again.*

Showing the reader she's engaged or married, rather than *telling* them

She glanced nervously in the mirror and adjusted it a fraction. The diamond on her left hand briefly caught the light as she changed gear. *Normal, normal, normal. Ordinary. It's a day like any other. It's a journey like any other. You've done this a hundred times before. Think about next week. Think about Alan. Think!*

Italics to indicate the character's thoughts

She looked in the mirror again.

A black car.

Something quivered inside her. *It was a coincidence – that was all. There must be a hundred black cars in the city, a thousand.* She gripped the wheel more tightly.

She looked in the mirror again.

Creative: short story	
Limited setting	
Definite shape or structure	
Few characters	
Action takes place over a relatively short space of time	
Limited number of plot 'events'	
Use of imagery, metaphor, simile, personification …	
Use of symbolism	
Provides insight into a character's life/thoughts/feelings	
Reveals or *shows* the reader things rather than telling them	
Use of believable dialogue to bring characters to life	
Credible ending	
Some sort of change evident (from the fortunes/situation/mind-set of the character(s) at the story's start)	
Spelling is consistently accurate	
Punctuation is consistently accurate	
Sentence construction is consistently accurate	

Stimulus for the reflection

Repeated structure emphasises what was important in his life

Appropriate use of imagery linked to mining

Relative Values

(reflective)

First draft

It's not much to look at: just a small lapel badge made up of the letters N.U.M.

National Union of Mineworkers; and yet every time I pick it up I am reminded of the man who wore it. A man with thirty years service 'man and boy' to his local pit. A man who loved the camaraderie of it all. A man who loved his pipe band and his football team. A man who loved his family – but never told them. Loyal to his union, to his mates, to his wife and children. Loyalty as much a part of him as the dust in his lungs that did for him in the end.

I peer down the dim shaft of time and try to see the man that he was but I can't. I sit at my laptop looking at his picture and I feel the accumulated years lying in layer upon layer between his youth and mine. And I think about the differences between us …

TOP TIP

In this kind of writing, make use of the techniques you have learned about as part of your study of prose fiction for the critical reading paper.

The writer introduces the idea that will be at the heart of this essay

Creative: reflective	
Captures the reader's interest	
Deals with a single idea/insight/experience	
Evidence of reflection on knowledge/thoughts/feelings caused by the subject of the essay	
Uses a personal tone	
The reader gets a clear sense of the writer's personality	
Gives a sense of the writer really *thinking* about the subject of the essay	
States what has been realised/learned by the writer	
Shows difference between how experience/event was viewed *then* and how it is viewed *now* (if appropriate)	
Uses word choice to create particular effects	
Uses imagery to create particular effects	
Uses sentence structure to create particular effects	
Spelling is consistently accurate	
Sentence construction is consistently accurate	

TOP TIP

Start writing your own blog. Use it as a way of sharing your reflections on your experiences.

Tempestuous Times – are wind farms a blot on the Scottish landscape?

(argumentative)

First draft

As we move further into the twenty-first century, it is clear that we must decide how our energy needs will be met in the coming years. At the moment we think nothing of switching on a light, a cooker, a computer – but how can we ensure that our insatiable demand for power can be satisfied in the future? Fossil fuels will disappear in 50 years according to some experts. That means no more power stations fuelled by coal or gas so it is vital that we find alternative means of generating electricity if that light, cooker and computer are still going to be available to us half a century from now.

Introductory paragraph sets out the context for the essay

Renewable forms of energy sources such as wind, wave and hydro will all play a significant role in providing us with energy in future. Will this mean more and more 'wind farms' being constructed in Scotland's countryside? Proponents of such schemes trumpet their 'eco-friendly' qualities whilst others warn against the damage that might be done to precious landscape. Which side is correct?

The Scottish Government want '80% of Scotland's gross annual electricity consumption' to come from renewable resources by 2020. Supporters of wind farms say that this means that we must build more turbines.

The two arguments that will be considered in the essay

Use of official statistics

Discursive: argumentative	
Introduces the topic clearly	
Makes use of *at least* two arguments related to the topic	
Has a clear, logical structure	
Makes effective use of linkage between sections/arguments	
Arguments supported by evidence (statistics etc.) where appropriate	
Effective use of transition markers (*however, furthermore, in addition to this, despite this* …)	
Uses an appropriate tone (conveyed through appropriate word choice and other language features)	
Uses comparisons	
Arguments disproved by evidence (statistics etc.) where appropriate	
Arrives at a clear conclusion having evaluated the evidence	
Spelling is consistently accurate	
Punctuation is consistently accurate	
Sentence construction is consistently accurate	
Sources consulted are clearly stated	

TOP TIP

In this kind of writing, remember to make use of the techniques you've learned about in the understanding and analysis unit and in work for the reading for understanding, analysis and evaluation exam paper.

Flatmates

(drama script)

First draft

Characters:

List of characters with brief outlines of personality and appearance

Claire – a well-dressed, tall, dark-haired young woman in her mid-twenties. She has the air of someone always in control. Her speech should sound 'educated' and precise.

Rebecca – the same age as Claire but shorter. Her demeanour suggests a very relaxed attitude to life in general.

Amy – prospective flatmate of Claire and Rebecca.

Stage directions to establish setting

It is a weekday morning in the living room of a flat in Glasgow. The room is clean and tidy. There is a sofa facing a wall on which there is a flat screen television above a fireplace. There are two 'modern' armchairs beside a coffee table. On the coffee table there is an open laptop and a (very) neatly stacked pile of magazines. The general impression is of orderliness. The only object which seems out of place is the empty beer can lying on its side on the floor beside the sofa.

Claire enters. She glances around the room, walks over to the coffee table and straightens the pile of magazines that does not need straightening. Once she is satisfied, she looks around the room once more, biting her lower lip.

Stage directions in italics

Claire: (*noticing the beer can on the floor*) Oh not again! (*shouting*) Becca! Get through here and look at this!

Rebecca: (*off*) What?

Characters' names down the left-hand margin

Claire: (*picks up the can and holds it distastefully at arm's length*) This! What sort of impression do you think this is going to make?

Rebecca enters. She is wearing a dressing gown. Her hair is unkempt and there is clear evidence of last night's make-up all over her face. She walks wearily past Claire. She studiously ignores Claire's outstretched arm, which still holds the beer can, and slumps into an armchair.

Claire: Well?

Rebecca: (eyes closed) Aw jeez, Claire. Get a life. What is it this time? Your IKEA catalogues no arranged in date order on the table? The curtains two centimetres too far apart?

Claire: Don't be like that! You know exactly what I am talking about.

Rebecca: (opening one eye and seemingly acknowledging the beer can for the first time) Oh, is that all? Ah thought it was something serious.

Claire: This *is* serious. You know she's coming round at ten thirty sharp. That means any minute now. Do I need to remind you how much we need a third to split the rent? Have you forgotten *why* the last one left?

Rebecca: (both eyes closed again) Och that could have happened to anyone. She was far too sensitive that yin! (both eyes open) Here, is it true she's still gettin' counsellin'?

The door bell rings. Claire exits and returns, ushering in Amy who is clearly nervous about the situation.

Costume suggests the character's personality

Dialogue suggests the character's personality

Effective use of humour

Creative: drama script (single scene)	
Stage directions	
Action limited to one setting	
Definite shape or structure	
Few characters	
Action takes place over a relatively short space of time	
Limited number of plot 'events'	
Lighting effects	
Sound effects	
Dialogue reveals characters' emotions, personalities, reactions etc.	
Climax or turning point in the action	
Satisfying ending (thought-provoking for the audience?)	
Spelling is consistently accurate	
Punctuation is consistently accurate	
Sentence construction is consistently accurate	
Script could be performed	

TOP TIP

Make a point of **watching** drama performances this year and look for techniques you could incorporate in your own script.

Ideas for writing

If you are stuck for inspiration, have a look at the following suggestions. They just might provide you with the inspiration to kick-start your writing. The more writing you do, the better you become at it. The opening lines are suggestions for practice pieces. Your teacher/assessor will give you further information about the writing and submission of pieces for the portfolio. Don't forget the importance of planning before you start!

Possible **titles** for short stories:

- Interiors
- Homecoming
- The Life and Times of Alexandra Macleod
- A Much Travelled Man
- New Year's Resolutions
- The Anti-social Network
- Waves
- Where the Dogs Howl
- An Inescapable Truth
- Daylight Robbery!
- The Examination
- Soldiers
- Wha's Like Us?
- The Road to Nowhere

Possible **opening lines** for short stories:

- John Smith caught, as he always did, the 7.58 to Paddington.
- I walk the line between our past and my present.
- Hergath watched the twin moons gradually appear above the horizon.
- She turned the key. Nothing. She turned the key again.
- The thrill of the chase is everything.
- I'm sitting at the same table in the same café at the same time of day. So far – no sign of him.
- The parcel on the doorstep was nothing special – just a slim cardboard box. What was inside, however, was anything but ordinary.
- Everyone disliked him. This was the simple truth. A simple truth in the same way that 'everyone has a father' is a simple truth – it could not be denied. He had long since stopped trying to deny it, even to himself.
- The adulation of the crowd had become essential to the girls. When they were on stage, nothing else mattered to them.
- 'Are we going to talk about this?'

  'What?'

  'You know fine what I mean.'

Possible topics for **argumentative** or **persuasive** pieces:

- The Edinburgh Tram Project.
- Scottish football referees should be awarded protected species status.
- Online 'friends' can never replace 'real' friends.
- Soap operas are a malign influence on our behaviour – we watch them at our peril.
- Wind farms are destroying our landscape.
- We should spend more money on transport systems.
- Why every Scottish city should be a green city.
- Schools should be more concerned with an individual's happiness than their academic achievement.
- What role does the church have in today's society?
- What can we do to reduce the ever-widening gulf between the rich and poor in our society?
- Do teenagers care about politics?
- Why is everyone so unpleasant to everyone else online?
- Computer gaming should be recognised for the complex entertainment art form it actually is.
- Female teachers are more effective than male teachers.
- Celebrities have forfeited their rights to privacy.
- The world of the same: why your town could be any town.

TOP TIP

Keep a writer's notebook and jot down things you overhear on the bus, in your local Starbucks, at a party … anything that you might incorporate in a story. Or keep the ideas as a memo or a recording on your phone.

Remember that it is advisable to choose a topic or issue you are interested in or feel strongly about. Try to avoid topics such as animal testing or abortion or size zero models unless you feel passionately about them and feel you will be able to write effectively about them. It will make the task, and your writing, so much better if the reader gets a sense of *your* engagement with the issue. Remember your writing needs to show **depth and complexity of thought**.

Possible scenarios for **drama scripts**:

- Two flatmates interview a third person to share with them.
- A dramatic monologue by a bus driver.
- A family gathering is disrupted by the revelation of a secret.
- Two strangers at a bus stop get talking and discover something in common.
- Three girls chat in a bar on a night out.
- A family argue in the departure lounge of an airport.
- A first date that goes wrong.
- A dramatic monologue by an O.A.P.
- A nervous employee is called into the boss's office.
- A check-out operator tries to make conversation with her customers.
- A parent tries to give their teenage child some 'good advice'.
- A passer-by comes into contact with a beggar on the street.
- Two football fans watch a game together and gradually reveal to the audience why they are addicted to their hobby.
- A taxi driver overhears one side of a mobile phone conversation with unpredictable results.
- A hill walking party gets lost and tensions within the group come to the surface.

Always bear in mind that a script is *designed to be performed*.

Ideas for **personal/reflective** writing:

It is difficult to suggest precise topics for personal reflective writing given the very personal nature of this kind of writing. You might like to think about the following possibilities.

- Reflect on your experiences as a young adult growing up in Scotland today.
- Think about an object that means a lot to you and reflect on why it is important.
- Think about how your personality has changed as you have grown older.
- Reflect on your experience of education to date.
- Reflect on your experience of love and relationships.
- What are the most important things in your life and why?
- Reflect on what you feel is the single most important experience in your life to date.
- Reflect on an experience that has changed the way you view the world.
- Reflect on your perception of religion and/or spirituality.
- Reflect on your experience of sport and/or competition.

Reading: Post-traumatic stress disorder is the invisible scar of war, pages 17–19

1. (a) Summarise in your own words the change in Stuart Tootal's attitude to PTSD. (*Outcome 1.2*)

    This should be a fairly straightforward question to answer. The passage says that the writer 'used to be sceptical' (paragraph 1) but that later his 'cynicism had disappeared'. Having located the appropriate parts of the passage, you then translate it into your own words. Your answer might look something like this:

    The writer did not really believe PTSD was important but now he is no longer scornful of it. The change happened because of his experiences leading soldiers in Afghanistan.

    (b) Analyse how the writer's language in these paragraphs conveys the reality of combat. (*Outcome 1.3*)

    To answer this question successfully you could comment on the writer's word choice, sentence structure and use of statistics. You could mention some of the following (remember to quote/refer to the word/technique and then comment on the connotations/effects).

    Word choice
    *   'intensive' (para 3) suggests the concentrated and demanding nature of the fighting.
    *   'Isolated' (para 3) suggests that the soldiers were very much on their own; difficult to summon support.
    *   'constant attack' (para 3) suggests the incessant nature of hostilities/no respite for the troops.
    *   'close-combat' (para 3) suggests almost hand-to-hand fighting.
    *   'increasing sophistication' (para 3) suggests the 'hi-tech' side to the war; that they were not fighting a primitive enemy.
    *   'enduring dread' (para 3) suggests ever-present fear.

    Sentence structure
    *   List (or triad) '... enemy assaults, mortars and rocket fire' highlights the variety of threats encountered by troops.

    Use of statistics
    *   'Fifteen of my battle group were killed in action ... 46 seriously wounded' suggests the high percentage of casualties sustained.

Re-read paragraph 4.

2. Analyse how the writer uses sentence structure and word choice to highlight the soldiers' experiences in Afghanistan and their experiences in the 'peacetime world'. (*Outcome 1.3*)

    In Afghanistan
    *   'valiantly' suggests their bravery.
    *   'admirably' suggests their reputations were enhanced.
    *   'constant stress' highlights the inescapable nature of the difficulties.
    *   Colon introduces the list of negative experiences 'loss of ... serious injury'.
    *   Use of contrasting ideas in the first sentence 'While we ... served valiantly ...' is juxtaposed with the realities of war 'loss of ... serious injury'.

- 'left a mark' this image suggests the psychological effects suffered by the soldiers – like a stain or a scar.

In the peacetime world

- 'readjusted ... reintegrated' contrasts with 'mental trauma'.
- 'deeply embedded' suggests how profound the problems are for sufferers of PTSD.
- Contrast in the final sentence: 'But while most of us ... for some ...' highlights the different outcomes for soldiers.

Re-read paragraphs 6–8.

3. What do you think might be a reason for the level of PTSD being 'slightly higher for infantry units and reservists'? (*Outcome 1.2*)

   *This question requires you to **infer** things from the passage. This is an important skill at Higher level. The passage won't actually give you the answer. Think carefully about what infantry are (and what they do) and how reservists are different from regular soldiers. Your answer might look like this:*

   'PTSD' might be higher for these groups because infantry come into contact with the enemy more directly and more frequently than other branches of the armed forces. Reservists are not full time soldiers and so might find it more difficult to deal with the realities of combat.

4. Identify and explain the writer's use of irony in paragraph 7. (*Outcome 1.3*)

   This is a straightforward question that tests your knowledge of irony. Remember to explain the effect.

   There is irony in the sentence which begins 'In 2012, 50 soldiers ...'. The irony lies in the fact that more soldiers killed themselves due to PTSD than were killed in combat. The writer makes use of irony to highlight the seriousness of the situation the veterans find themselves in.

5. Explain in your own words the **four** main points the writer makes in paragraph 8. (*Outcome 1.2*)

   This is another straightforward question asking you to identify some of the main ideas in the passage. Remember to 'locate' and 'translate'. Your answer might say

   The writer thinks

   - We should look again at the numbers ('review the statistics') of soldiers suffering from PTSD.
   - We should improve the help offered ('address the gaps in provision').
   - We should avoid making too much of the psychological effects of combat.
   - We should not judge those suffering from it.

Re-read paragraph 11.

6. The writer describes PTSD as 'an invisible scar of war.' Explain the meaning of this image and analyse its effect. (*Outcome 1.3*)

   This is a very common type of question in your unit assessment for Reading. Remember to say what is being compared to what. You can then say something about the effect of the image.

   The image compares PTSD to a mark left by a physical wound to the body that cannot be seen. It is effective because it describes a psychological injury in terms of a physical one – reminding us that one is just as damaging and long lasting as the other. Through using this image, the writer stresses the seriousness of PTSD.

Consider the text as a whole.

7. What evidence is there in the passage of the support offered to serving soldiers and veterans? Answer in your own words. (*Outcome 1.2*)

   There are a lot of things mentioned in the passage. You could refer to

Answers

- Strategies have been put in place by the MOD for when soldiers return from tours of duty in a combat zone.
- Soldiers are taught about the condition.
- Charities attempt to deal with PTSD.
- Civilian employers have special programmes for veterans.

Again the important thing is to use your own words when the question demands it.

8. Identify a purpose of this text. Explain your answer with close reference to the text. (*Outcome 1.1*)

   You've got a bit of freedom with this one – the question refers to 'a purpose' so any reasonable purpose supported by evidence from the text will do. You might say any one of the following:

   - To raise awareness of PTSD.
   - To highlight the reality of what serving in combat means.
   - To show what can be done to help victims of PTSD.

   Whichever one you go for, support your answer by quoting or referring to the text, e.g.

   To highlight the reality of what serving as a soldier in a combat zone means – 'constant attack from enemy assaults'; 'constant stress of facing death'.

9. A text may have many audiences. Identify a possible audience for this text, and explain your answer with close reference to the text. (*Outcome 1.1*)

   Again there are a number of possible answers to this. Ask yourself who might choose to read this article. Possible answers might include:

   - Someone interested in the military.
   - Someone interested in psychological illness.
   - Someone interested in politics.
   - The general reader.

The important thing is to support your answer by quoting/referring to the text.

Listening: Practice listening assessment, pages 20–21

1. What is Michael Billington's opinion of David Tennant's performance as Hamlet and how is this opinion conveyed through his language?

   He likes it/is positive about it.

   Conveyed by:

   - *Listing all the positive features of Tennant's performance 'manic, quicksilver restless energy, a fierce intelligence and a lot of wit and humour'. This suggests he likes the cleverness and liveliness of Tennant's performance.*
   - *He uses alliteration 'compelling and compulsive' to describe Tennant's Hamlet, which suggests the enthralling and gripping nature of the performance.*

2. What is another reason for the success of this production of *Hamlet*?

   The quality of the supporting cast.

3. What is Michael Billington's opinion of what it means to play Dr Who, as opposed to Hamlet, and how is this conveyed through his language?

   He thinks it's much more challenging to play Hamlet.

   Conveyed by:

   - *He uses a musical metaphor saying that Dr Who is a 'five finger exercise' — a practice exercise for piano. This suggests that he thinks playing the part of the Doctor is just a basic, repetitive task. He then says that in comparison to that, Hamlet is a 'rich piano concerto', which suggests it takes a lot of skill. The word 'rich' suggests there is much more variety and potential depth to the role.*
   - *He also says that Hamlet tests all of an actor's skills ('requires every single acting muscle a performer can give'), which further suggests the demanding nature of the part.*

4. What does Simon Russell Beale mean when he says that Hamlet is 'quite hospitable as a part'?

   He means that it is so demanding that it is impossible to give the perfect performance of the part ('You're never going to get it all right') and so this actually takes some of the pressure off — actors can only do their best in the role ('bring what I can to it').

5. How does Simon Russell Beale's language help to convey the idea of 'hundreds of different types of Hamlets'?

   Use of repetition/contrasts — 'very gentle to very savage'; 'very witty'/'very serious' suggests the wide range of possible interpretations of the part.

6. Analyse how Michael Billington's use of language helps to emphasise the fact that this production is about more than just David Tennant as Hamlet.

   His word choice 'rich complex network' suggests all the characters are linked in an intricate fashion and that this is an important element of the play as a whole.

   You'll note that Michael Billington uses the word 'rich' repeatedly in this discussion!

7. Analyse Simon Russell Beale's description of what it is like to have played Hamlet.

   He uses a simile 'as if you've joined a rather nice club', which suggests that the actors who have managed to play the part then become part of some exclusive (and perhaps privileged) group.

8. What conclusion is reached at the end of the discussion?

   That actors can 'cross over' successfully from one branch of acting to another and that this has been going on for a long time.

Answers

9. Identify the **purpose** of this extract and explain why you think this, based on what you have heard in the extract.

    You might mention any one of the following. Always remember to support your answer with evidence from the extract.

    - To review David Tennant's performance.
    - To discuss whether actors can move from one branch of acting to another.
    - To discuss what it means to play Hamlet.
    - To review the new production of Hamlet.

10. Identify one possible **audience** for the extract and explain why you think this, based on what you have heard in the extract.

    You might suggest any of the following:

    - Fans of David Tennant.
    - People interested in the theatre or Shakespeare.
    - Students of drama.
    - People interested in celebrities.
    - The general listener.
    - Older, educated people (typical Radio 4 listeners).

    Or any other reasonable possible audience.

    Again the important thing is to support the answer with evidence from the text.

How to study poetry: Asking questions about poems, 'Heliographer', page 31

1. What is the poem about?

   The poem seems to be about a child (a young boy?) looking down on his home town with his father. As he does so he learns how to drink from a bottle of lemonade. The poem seems to be about growing up — it describes a particular 'rite of passage' as the boy learns to do something in the way 'grown-ups' do. The title 'Heliographer' and the word 'decoded' suggest that the poem might also be saying something about signs and signals. What do you think?

2. Who is speaking?

   The young boy or the grown man he has become who is looking back on the incident.

3. How is the poem structured?

   The poem is divided into two stanzas, one of eight lines and one of six. The division into eight and six suggests it is a kind of sonnet although it doesn't have a sonnet's rhyme scheme. There does seem to be a change at the volta when his father intervenes. What do you think?

4. What other techniques have been used?

   Word choice/imagery

   - 'decoded' has connotations of the father reading and explaining to the boy the landscape spread out below the two of them. It also echoes the title, 'Heliographer' — a signaller who transmitted messages in Morse code by reflecting the sun's rays in a mirror. Armies used heliographers to send signals on the battlefield before the invention of radio.
   - 'bolted' describes the boy's attempts to drink from the bottle as if it is some mechanical operation.
   - 'shaky/single-handed grip' suggests the effort needed by the boy. As well as now only needing one hand to complete the task, there are also connotations of doing something on your own in the phrase 'single-handed' — the act of drinking from the bottle becomes a symbol of the boy's increasing independence.
   - 'it detonated with light' suggests something explosive (violent?) and sudden as the sun's rays catch the bottle.

   Simile

   'my lips pursed like a trumpeter's' continues the idea of sending signals introduced earlier in the poem.

   Sound

   Onomatopoeia: 'Clunk', 'butted' suggests the boy's clumsiness.

   Sentence structure

   The triad of 'our tenement, the rival football grounds, / the long bridges', which suggests the setting for the incident described (it seems they are looking down from Dundee Law). The movement from home (the tenement) to the football grounds and then to the bridges suggest the boy's future progression in life and that he will grow up and ultimately leave the city.

5. How effective are the poet's methods in conveying the meaning of the text to the reader?

   The poet's methods are effective in conveying the central concerns of this text. The short, compact form he has chosen for the poem effectively brings a brief moment in time to life. The word choice and imagery suggest the significance of the incident in the speaker's growing up. The allusions to signs and symbols add a further layer of meaning to the poem.

6. What is your personal reaction to the poem?

   You will have responded to the poem in your own way. Did you like the way this incident was described? It seems a skilful evocation of a childhood experience.

How to study poetry: Asking questions about poems, 'In a snug room', page 31

1. What is the poem about?

   A successful businessman enjoys a drink in a bar. He thinks about his recent successes. He awaits the arrival of his 'true love'. MacCaig suggests he is about to be punished for his complacency.

2. Who is speaking?

   A detached, neutral poetic voice. Perhaps the poet himself.

3. How is the poem structured?

   - The concise form of the poem adds impact to its message.
   - Free verse with no regular rhythm or rhyme for most of the poem suits the 'mini-narrative' MacCaig is telling us.
   - Movement in the poem from the comfortable (literal and metaphorical) position of the anonymous man to the idea that his life is about to fall apart.

4. What other techniques have been used?

   Word choice/imagery

   - 'snug' suggests 'sheltered'; 'cosy'; 'comfortable' (you might even have heard of the old expression 'as snug as a bug in a rug'!). 'The snug' is also the name for a separate room in an old-fashioned bar, which makes it doubly apt in this context – 'snug' refers to both the setting of the poem and how the subject of the poem feels in the first stanza.
   - 'He' suggests his anonymity but he is clearly a man of some importance; someone with a public profile ('flattering reference...morning papers').
   - 'sips' suggests a measure of sophistication or refinement.
   - 'complacently' suggests he is self-satisfied or perhaps smug.
   - 'cronies' implies close friends (although 'cronyism' now has negative connotations and a sense of corruption).
   - 'profitable' suggests he's a successful businessman (a fat cat? A banker?).
   - 'donation' suggests his philanthropic side – his generosity. Or is he just salving a guilty conscience?
   - 'And he smiles ...' suggests further complacency – the day just seems to be getting better and better for this man. Notice how the poet deliberately leaves us guessing as to the identity of his 'true love'. Who's coming? His wife? His mistress? Someone (or something) else? 'true love' seems a rather old-fashioned expression.
   - Reference to 'Nemesis' gives this concise narrative a sense of 'universality' – we are invited to read it as a modern morality tale; especially when we take into account the anonymity of the central character.

   Sentence structure

   - Colon introduces the list of things he is pleased with.

   Sound

   - Alliteration ('deal...dotted...donation') the repeated hard plosive 'd' sounds help to suggest the certainty of the hard-headed businessman.

- Concluding rhyme ('gun'/'one') helps to underline the final message of the poem: a warning to the self-satisfied. You might argue that this seems a peculiarly 'Scottish' response to those who are successful!
- The word 'gun' echoes the word 'snug' in the title (Seamus Heaney does exactly the same in his poem 'Digging').

Other features include

- Placing line 10 in a line on its own:
  - ➤ allows the poet to sum up succinctly the seemingly 'perfect' day being enjoyed by the man
  - ➤ allows a dramatic pause before the climax of the poem.
- Placing the closing lines in a separate stanza provides a dramatic conclusion to the poem.
- Witty juxtaposition of ancient and modern (Greek goddess and 'two bullets …').

5. How effective are the poet's methods in conveying the meaning of the text to the reader?

    The techniques outlined above all convey the meaning of the text effectively. The poem offers a blunt warning against being overly complacent and smug about your life and/or yourself.

6. What is your personal reaction to the poem?

    Do you like this poem or not? Do you feel sorry for the man?

The age of the amateur has passed, by Ed Smith, pages 42–43

1. In the past it was a fashionable concept (1) but now it is looked down on as out of date nonsense (1).
2. The positioning of a cricketer's initials (1). The manner in which professionals had to address amateur players who were not as good as them (1).
3. It permitted a wide range of different types of people to be included/It promoted a person's unique talents (1) and it gave people more freedom (1).
4. They come from the elements of our characters (1) that can't be worked out logically (1).
5. They are successful because they don't have too much familiarity with their sport (1) and they don't think about their performance too much (1).

Dangerous liaisons, by Lucy Mangan, pages 52–53

See how many of the following features you spotted.

'What you have instead in Meyer's work is a **depressingly retrograde, deeply anti-feminist, borderline misogynistic** novel that drains its heroine of life and vitality as surely **as if a vampire had sunk his teeth into her and leaves her a bloodless cipher** while the story happens around her. Edward tells her she is 'so interesting ... fascinating', but the reader **looks in vain** for his evidence.'

- *List of three highly critical descriptions of the work ('depressingly retrograde ... borderline misogynistic').*
- *Emotive word choice: 'depressingly'.*
- *Appropriate use of vampire image to reinforce the writer's opinion of the poor characterisation in the novel.*
- *'bloodless cipher' image suggests the character is not portrayed as someone the reader can engage with.*
- *'looks in vain' suggests it's a hopeless task.*

'**Alas**, the **only choice** Bella gets to make is to sacrifice herself in ever-larger increments ...'

- *'Alas ...' suggests Mangan's disappointment.*
- *'only choice' suggests the constraints placed on Bella.*

'It sounds **melodramatic and shrill** to say that Bella and Edward's relationship is abusive, **but as the story wears on it becomes increasingly hard to avoid the comparison ...**'

- *'melodramatic and shrill' shows Mangan acknowledges that some people might think she is going too far in her criticism. In the second half of the sentence she justifies this word choice.*

'To **those less enamoured of Meyerworld** ...'

- *'those less enamoured' a good example of understatement.*
- *'Meyerworld' seems dismissive – hints at a version of society that Mangan disagrees with.*

'The **few signs of wit and independence** ...'

- *Again, highly critical of the character suggesting there is little indication of the sort of qualities Mangan expects in a female central character.*

'**mute devotion**'

- *Suggests a passive, silent follower or disciple.*

'**slavish**'

- *Suggests Bella's lack of freedom in the relationship.*

'**Edward is no hero. Bella is no Buffy.**'

- *Parallel sentence structures again underlining how Mangan feels Twilight suffers in comparison with Buffy.*
- *Short sentences add impact.*
- *Alliteration in the second sentence draws our eye to the sentence and reinforces the point being made.*

'And *Twilight's* underlying message – that self-sacrifice makes you a worthy girlfriend, that men mustn't be excited beyond a certain point, that men with problems must be forgiven everything, that female passivity is a state to be encouraged **– are no good to anyone**. **It should be staked through its black, black heart.**'

- Parenthesis (inside paired dashes) is a list of what Mangan considers to be the negative message conveyed by the book and film.
- It's followed by the brief and blunt statement 'are no good to anyone'.
- Final sentence contains another appropriate vampire image as Mangan suggests the Twilight phenomenon should be killed off in the same way a vampire is.
- Repetition of 'black' also serves to emphasise Mangan's (perhaps rather exaggerated) point that Twilight is almost something evil.

Close Reading exam paper, questions on passage 1, 'Only a Theory', pages 61–62

1.	Read lines 1– 6. According to the writer why is teaching Roman history and the Latin language a 'big undertaking' (lines 5) and what does this require from the teacher?	4
	This is a straightforward 'understanding' type question so **locate** *and then* **translate** *the appropriate words in the passage.*	
	1 mark if you made the general point that it's because of the wide range or complexity of topics to be covered and 1 mark each for any two of the following examples of that wide range:	
	• Poetry (the 'elegiacs' and 'odes' mentioned in the passage).	
	• Language structure ('grammar').	
	• Roman conflicts or battles (you should be able to gloss 'wars' even if you've never heard or read the word 'Punic' before — remember you will encounter unfamiliar vocabulary in this exam).	
	• Roman leaders (the 'Julius Caesar' reference).	
	• Luxurious and corrupt lives of rulers (a gloss of 'voluptuous excesses').	
	and 1 mark for recognising	
	• The significant commitment/attention/focus/application/devotion required by the teacher (gloss of 'time, concentration, dedication').	
2.	Analyse the writer's use of language in lines 6–10 to convey what he feels about the threat posed by the 'ignoramuses' (line 7).	2
	Remember that any reference to the writer's 'use of language' in a question should trigger a checklist of features and techniques to start running through your mind (word choice, imagery, structure, tone, sound …). In a question like this you can score 2 marks for an 'insightful' or well-expressed point about a single feature. What makes a comment 'insightful'? It's all to do with how perceptive your understanding of the technique the writer is using seems to be and how well you express any comment about it. It's always safer to make more than one point in a two-mark question! You need to refer to (and quote) an appropriate feature or technique and then comment on it.	
	For this question you can score up to 2 marks for a single well expressed point. 1 mark for each more basic point. A 'reference alone' (just pointing out a feature or technique without a comment) does not score any marks (0). Each of the possible answers set out below consists of a reference and then a suggested comment.	
	Imagery (remember to explain the 'root' of the image in your answer):	
	• Baying pack of hounds chasing their quarry.	
	• Preyed upon predators attacking weaker animals.	
	Word choice:	
	• 'baying' — loud/menacing.	
	• 'ignoramuses' — anti-intellectual/uncivilised.	
	• 'scurry about' — animal like/unattractive/secretive/busybodies.	
	• 'tirelessly' — never giving up.	
	Sound:	
	• Alliteration — 'precious', 'preyed' catches the eye (or ear) and helps to underline the point the writer is making.	

3.	Referring to specific language features, how effective do you find lines 14–17 as a conclusion to the opening paragraph?	4
	In answering a question like this you need to make sure that the features you identify and comment on relate back to what has gone before in the paragraph.	
	Up to 2 marks for a sophisticated analysis of any one feature. 1 mark for a more basic point. For full marks structure and word choice must be covered.	
	Possible answers	
	Sentence structure:	
	• Balanced structure ('Instead of devoting … , you are forced to …') highlights time wasted on answering attacks.	
	• Colon introduces expansion of the idea of the 'rearguard defence'.	
	Word choice:	
	• 'noble vocation' — higher calling/emphasises status of the Latin teacher.	
	• 'rearguard defence' — desperately fighting off attackers.	
	• 'make you weep' — suggests sense of despair engendered by ignorant attacks.	
	• 'exhibition' — shows their lack of self-awareness/sense of proportion.	
	• 'ignorant' sums up critics' — lack of knowledge.	
	• 'prejudice' — shows unthinking response/base instinct.	
	Tone:	
	• *You could also make the point that the tone of these lines (one of anger, despair or exasperation at the 'ignoramuses') is in keeping with the rest of the paragraph and support it with reference to any of the language features outlined above.*	
4.	According to the writer, what are the characteristics of the 'Holocaust-deniers' (line 21)?	2
	*This is another **locate** and **translate** question.*	
	1 mark each for a successful gloss of any two of:	
	• 'vocal' — promote their message (not just 'loud').	
	• 'superficially plausible' — believable on a very simplistic level.	
	• 'adept at seeming learned' — skilled at appearing intellectual/academic.	
5.	By referring to at least two features of language in lines 25–30, analyse how the writer conveys his disapproval of the situation faced by the hypothetical history teacher.	4
	*This is another question where the words **features of language** should trigger that checklist of features and techniques in your mind. Below are possible comments you could have made on word choice, punctuation and structure.*	
	*You would score up to 2 marks for a sophisticated analysis of any one feature. 1 mark for a more basic point. For full marks **two** language features must be covered.*	
	• 'continually faced with' — incessant nature of problem.	
	• 'belligerent' — aggressive.	
	• Inverted commas around 'equal time' highlight the writer's feeling that this is a waste of time.	
	• Inverted commas around 'the controversy' and 'alternative theory' suggest the lack of status he awards these ideas.	

- Inverted commas around 'respected' highlight his own lack of respect for the idea.
- 'Fashionably relativist' — trendy/lacking certainty/clarity.
- 'chime in' — irritating addition to the debate.
- Colon and semi-colon used to structure the relativist intellectuals' argument that 'all points of view are equally valid'.

6.	Read lines 31–41. Analyse the writer's use of language in this paragraph to highlight his feelings of sympathy for science teachers today. You should refer in your answer to such features as word choice, sentence structure, imagery …	4

This question helpfully reminds you of the sort of language features to comment on.

Up to 2 marks for a sophisticated analysis of any one feature. 1 mark for a more basic point. For full marks two language features must be covered.

Possible answers

Structure:

- Repetition 'when they … when they … when they …' shows the extent of their efforts.
- List of good they do separated by semi-colons.
- Balanced structure of second sentence in the paragraph (contrast between positive efforts followed by description of obstacles).
- Repeated structures with contrasting meanings: 'explore and explain'/'harried and stymied'/'hassled and bullied'.
- Repetition 'They are …' suggests the variety of difficulties faced.
- Contrast 'Once … now …'.

Word choice:

- 'honestly' — shows their integrity.
- 'very nature of life itself' — dealing with fundamental issues.
- 'harried' — chased.
- 'stymied' — obstructed/blocked.
- 'hassled' — bothered.
- 'bullied/threatened/menacing' — putting pressure on the teacher.
- 'wasted at every turn' — consistently interfered with.
- 'sarcastic smirks' — negative attitude of pupils/belittling teacher's efforts.
- 'close-folded arms' — body language mirrors 'closed' minds.
- 'brainwashed' — as if indoctrinated/conditioned.
- 'state-approved' — big-brother society.
- 'systematically expunged' — methodically/deliberately removed from the textbooks.
- 'bowdlerized' — altered from the original/loss of original sense or true meaning.

Punctuation:

- Inverted commas around 'change over time' suggests it is a less precise expression than 'evolution' OR inverted commas are used simply because he is quoting from a 'politically correct' textbook and wishes the reader to share his outrage at the use of the term.

7.	Reread lines 50–59. By referring to at least one example, analyse how the writer's use of imagery reinforces his view of those who hold creationist beliefs.	**2**
	Remember to explain the 'root' of the image – say what is being compared to what. Make sure you justify why you think it is effective (or not).	
	Up to 2 marks for a detailed/insightful comment. 1 mark for a more basic response.	
	Creating the universe is compared to starting an engine (which runs by itself thereafter). 'Cranked' doesn't sound like a particularly 'high-tech' piece of engineering. It is effective because the image allows the writer to poke (gentle) fun at those who hold such beliefs. This lends weight to the writer's own theory.	
	Or	
	The beginning of the universe is compared to some sort of baptism ceremony ('solemnized its birth'). The writer clearly thinks this sort of personification is the wrong way to think about the universe.	
8.	Analyse the writer's use of language in the final paragraph to emphasise his position on this subject.	**3**
	Look carefully at the final paragraph. What aspects of language did you spot?	
	Up to 2 marks for an insightful comment on one feature. 1 mark for a more basic comment.	
	Possible answers:	
	• Short, blunt first sentence states case clearly.	
	• Repetition of 'Beyond ... Beyond ...' shows the extent of the case for evolution/irrefutable quality of the evidence.	
	• 'Beyond sane, informed, intelligent doubt' – triad of adjectives effectively shows the quality of the evidence for his argument.	
	• Repetition of 'fact' to drive home the certainty he has.	
	• Repetition of 'cousins ...' to emphasise the inter-related nature of all species.	
	• 'somewhat more distant ... more distant ... still ... yet more distant ...' suggests the breadth of the evolutionary process.	
	• Cumulative effect of 'not self-evidently, tautologically, obviously true'.	
	• Final sentence ends with simple statement reinforcing the writer's case.	

Close Reading exam paper, question on both passages, pages 63–64

Question on both passages

Both writers express their views about the teaching of evolution and creationism. Identify key areas on which they disagree. In your answer, you should refer in detail to both passages.

The mark for this question should reflect the quality of response in two areas:

- *Identification of the key areas of agreement/disagreement in attitude/ideas.*
- *Level of detail given in support.*

To answer this, look again at where the writers seem to disagree. For example, what do they say about the status of creationism and evolution as theories that are taught in schools? Do they both believe that science teachers should 'correct' students who have creationist views? What is their opinion of those with a 'creationist' world view?

Marks are allocated as follows:

5 marks – comprehensive identification of three or more key areas of disagreement with full use of supporting evidence.

4 marks – clear identification of three or more key areas of disagreement with relevant use of supporting evidence.

3 marks – identification of three or more key areas of disagreement with supporting evidence.

2 marks – identification of two key areas of disagreement with supporting evidence.

1 mark – identification of one key area of disagreement with supporting evidence.

0 marks – failure to identify any key area of disagreement and/or total misunderstanding of task.

5

Drama: *The Slab Boys*, by John Byrne, pages 68–71

	Answers	
1.	By referring closely to lines 1–16, show how the play's setting in time is established for the audience. *You should refer to the following:* • *Spanky's hairstyle and costume ('drainpipe trousers', 'Tony Curtis Hairdo', 'crepe soled shoes') suggests the 'uniform' of a 1950s Teddy Boy.* • *The use of the word 'wireless'.* • *The reference to 'Luxemburg', the pirate radio station.* • *The reference to 'Terry Dene' singing 'A White Sports Coat', a popular song of the day. This (originally American) song suggests the influence of American pop culture on Britain at the time.* *These all serve to (very economically) establish the action of the play firmly in the 1950s, with the obvious influence of American culture.*	3
2.	By referring to two examples of dialogue in this extract, show how the playwright establishes the character of Willie Curry. *The key point to make is that he is presented almost as a caricature or stereotype of the older authority figure, forever bemoaning the behaviour of those younger than him and always harking back to a better time. This is illustrated through dialogue such as:* • *'If I'd had you chaps out in Burma' marks him as being of the older generation who served in the war. It suggests he feels less powerful now and is nostalgic for the army discipline he could administer in the past.* • *'silly duck's arse haircut'/'bloody contraption'/'that racket'/'gadget' suggest his dismissive contempt for current styles and technology.* • *'you're for the high jump' typical of his clichéd authoritarian threats.* • *'Now get on with it …' typical of the orders he gives.*	3

3.	Analyse the effect of some of the different registers of language in dialogue spoken by the characters that are evident in this extract.
	
	To answer this you could refer to:
	
	• *The earthy coarseness of lines such as 'Dee-oh-raw-ho … the skitters' for humorous effect and which help to establish Phil's character.*
	• *The use of Scots idiom/dialect to establish the setting of the play and the working class background of the characters.*
	    ➤ *'Who belongs to the Juke Box?'*
	    ➤ *'… no what you'd cry a spectator sport'*
	    ➤ *'could you not've brung in'*
	    ➤ *'my maw's Christmas present'*
	• *Phil and Spanky's imitation of the language of English public school stories in lines: 'Bless my boater, did you catch that, Cherry? A yuletide cadeau for the squirt's mater …' for humorous effect but also as a marker of the theme of class and privilege that is revealed as one of the play's concerns.*
	• *Words taken from American popular culture such as 'vamoose' (Western).*
		4

Answers

4.	By referring to this extract and elsewhere in the play, discuss how the theme of bullying is developed in the text.	**10**
	You can answer this question in bullet points or in a series of linked statements.	
	Marks are allocated to this question (as they are for all the 10-mark Scottish text questions) as follows:	
	You will get up to 2 marks for identifying an area of 'commonality' – in this case you could refer to the fact the bullying (of Hector and Alan) in the extract is then developed in the treatment Hector receives at the hands of Phil and Spanky later in the play.	
	There are another 2 marks available for referring to the extract – you could discuss the business with the radio and Spanky's breaking of the aerial callously dismissing the fact that it was supposed to be a present for Hector's 'maw'. You might also identify that the suggestion of 'cufflinks' as a replacement present is another cruel jibe at Hector's expense (although also one designed to raise a laugh from the audience). You could point out Phil and Spanky's deliberate use of the wrong names for Alan –'Archie', 'Andy', 'Eamonn', 'Alec' – in order to make him feel unwelcome.	
	Whatever references you choose to make, remember to comment on their effect.	
	The remaining 6 marks are allocated for your comments on other parts of the text and how they convey the theme of bullying. Effective and insightful comments will always score well. Markers will award 3, 2 or 1 marks to each point that you make. For this question you might refer to and comment on Phil and Spanky's treatment of Hector and Alan:	
	• 'He was going to be a Capucci monk' – they suggest Hector is Catholic.	
	• Alan's Parker pen is taken off him.	
	• Phil and Spanky make fun of Hector's Uncle Bertie.	
	• Phil and Spanky make fun of Hector's intention of taking Lucille to the staff dance.	
	• The casual cruelty in their description of Hector 'Everything's wrong with you ...'.	
	• The cutting of Hector's ear.	
	• The 'new' look created for Hector.	
	There are many other episodes in the play that you could refer to.	

Prose: *Sunset Song*, by Lewis Grassic Gibbon, pages 72–73

	Answers	
1.	By close reference to paragraphs 1 and 2, explain how the writer's language conveys a sense of Marget Strachan's character. *In your answer you could refer to and comment on some of the following:* • List of adjectives to describe her 'slim and sweet and fair' emphasises her attractive qualities — (deliberate) echo of a description that we might find in an old folk tale or ballad. • This description is contrasted by the 'awful things' (sex and reproduction) she speaks about — she is much more 'worldly wise' than Chris. • She is ambitious ('off to be trained as a doctor') and practical — she won't wait for the arrival of her father's 'Revolution'. • The comparison used in the description of her eyes, 'blue and so deep they reminded you of a well you peered into', suggests her attractive/mysterious qualities. • These qualities are emphasised by the alliteration in the comparatives 'deeper and darker'. • Grassic Gibbon contrasts the 'solemn' and serious side of her nature with the much more light-hearted side 'laughing and fleering'. The overall impression is of a bright, lively and attractive individual. *You would be awarded up to 2 marks for a detailed or insightful comment you made and 1 mark for a more basic comment. Remember the marks are allocated for your* **comment on the effect** *of each feature that you identify. There are no marks just for identifying a language feature.*	4
2.	By referring to at least two examples from paragraph 3, analyse how the writer conveys a sense of the contrast between life and death. *You could refer to any of the following. The question asks about a contrast so for full marks you must offer comment on the features that refer to life and to death.* Life • Sensory experience and an acute sense of being alive suggested by the list of adjectives 'Clean and keen and wild and clear'. • Grassic Gibbon's description of 'the vein that beat in Marget's throat, a little blue gathering' suggests how small and fragile life is. • 'blood beat past in slow quiet strokes' — the alliteration and the short simple words suggest the pulse of life. • More vivid sensory experience suggested by the descriptions 'lowe of burning whins' and 'hearing the North Sea thunder beyond the hills'. • Repetition of 'thunder' to highlight the contrast with the 'dark silence' of death. • 'morning of mist' has connotations of something transitory and insubstantial. Death • 'dead and still under grass' contrasts with the lively picture created of life above ground. • 'you'd never smell' suggests the finality of death. • 'cased' suggests being confined and enclosed. • 'icy darkness' suggests something forbidding and frightening.	4

Answers

3.	By referring to two examples from Paragraphs 3 and 4, analyse how the writer conveys Chris's perception of the incident with Marget.	2
	Here you could refer to:	
	Word choice	
	• 'red' suggests both passion and life.	
	• 'kind' suggests this was not an aggressive act.	
	• 'over in a moment', 'quick' suggests transitory nature of experience.	
	• 'shameful' suggests something wrong, illicit.	
	• 'fine/tingling/shameful' effectively suggest the conflicting emotions felt by Chris.	
	Comparison	
	• 'so red they were they looked like haws' another example of Chris seeing things in terms of the natural world.	
	Sentence structure	
	• Repetition/triad 'lovely ... lovely ... lovelier'.	
	• Dashes indicate the different stages of Marget's actions as she prepares to kiss Chris.	
	• Long, climactic build up to '... and kiss you like this!'	
	Again you must remember to comment fully on your chosen examples.	
4.	This extract refers to two aspects of Chris's character. By referring to this extract and from elsewhere in the novel, discuss how Grassic Gibbon conveys these aspects of Chris's character.	10
	You can answer this question in bullet points or in a series of linked statements.	
	Marks are allocated to this question (as they are for all the 10-mark Scottish text questions) as follows:	
	You will get up to 2 marks for identifying an area of 'commonality' – in this case you could refer to the fact that this extract refers to the 'Two Chrisses' – the English Chris and the Scots Chris – and that this 'divided' Chris is also evident in other parts of the novel such as when she is torn between going off to train as a teacher when her father dies or staying and taking over the running of the croft.	
	There are another 2 marks available for referring to the extract – you could refer to the word choice in the description of Chris and her thoughts in the first paragraph:	
	English Chris	
	'douce and studious'	
	Scots Chris	
	'sat back'	
	'laughed a canny laugh'	
	'antics of the teachers'	
	You could also refer to the list 'champ of horses/smell of dung/father's brown grained hands', which suggests her affinity with the land and those who work on it.	
	'sick to be home again' suggests the strength of her feelings for the land.	
	Whatever references you choose to make, remember to comment on their effect.	

The remaining 6 marks are allocated for your comments on other parts of the text and how they convey the two aspects of Chris's character. Effective and insightful comments will always score well. Markers will award 3, 2 or 1 marks to each point that you make. For this question you might refer to and comment on:

- Her love/admiration for her father and her fear of him.
- When she is torn between going off to train as a teacher when her father dies or staying and taking over the running of the croft.
- The calm and collected way she deals with her relatives and the lawyer and her fight with Ewan in Seed Time.

There are many other episodes in the novel you could refer to.

Poetry: *Nil Nil*, by Donald Paterson, pages 74–75

Answers

1.	By referring to specific features, explain how this extract relates to the earlier parts of the poem. *In your answer you could mention:* - 'Unknown to him' echoes the 'abandoned histories' and the idea of 'deeper and deeper obscurity'. - 'him' refers to Horace Madden, mentioned in the first narrative. - 'it' refers to the stone he kicks into the gutter, which is revealed in this extract to be the pilot's gallstone. - References to place names: 'Leuchars', 'Tayport', 'Carnoustie', 'Sidlaws', echo the references to the Dundee area in the first narrative. - 'the Sidlaws unsheathed from their great black tarpaulin' repeats the image in the epigraph 'imagine the vast, rustling map of Burgundy, say, settling over it like a freshly starched sheet!'	3
2	By referring closely to lines 4–16, analyse the use of poetic technique to describe the fighter pilot's experience. *To answer this question you might comment on some of the following:* Word choice - 'lone (fighter-pilot)' suggests his isolation and/or his heroic status. - 'unsheathed' suggests the hills emerge like knives or swords; suggests something threatening the pilot. - 'unscheduled' suggests the unexpected nature of his emergency. - 'flurry' suggests the socks streaming into the sky. - 'rendered' suggests something given up as an offering to someone. - 'irenicon' suggests something used to secure peace — offers a contrast to the ideas contained in 'fighter pilot'.	4

Answers

		Imagery	

Imagery
- 'their great black tarpaulin' suggests the hills are covered in dark mist or fog. This image echoes the reference to the giant map laid over Burgundy in the epigraph. The image also has sinister connotations of something shrouded.
- 'twirling away like an ash-key' suggests the helplessness of the pilot as the plane spirals to the ground.
- 'like a sackful of doves' conventional symbols of peace.

Sound
- Onomatopoeia 'plopped' — faintly childish or ridiculous word contrasting with the seriousness of the engine failure.

Tone
- The mix of the serious and the comic makes the reader consider anew and question the significance of Paterson's description of the pilot's experience in terms of the central concerns of the poem as a whole.

You might get up to 2 marks for a detailed, insightful comment on one feature. You will always get 1 mark for a more basic, accurate comment. Remember that there are no marks for reference/quotation alone.

3. Evaluate how effective you find lines 16–21 of this extract. Your answer should deal with ideas and/or language. **3**

*To answer this you should refer to specific features of the text and comment on them. The question asks you to **evaluate** so make sure you make some sort of statement about the lines being effective or very effective or fairly effective and then give your evidence to support your evaluative statement.*

You could mention:
- The cartoon-like (but still gruesome) image of the pilot and his plane hitting the ground at the same time.
- 'made nothing of him' reminds the reader of the central concerns of this poem — the idea of loss/decline/nothingness. There is also humorous allusion in the expression.
- The list — 'fillings', 'tackets', 'lucky half crown', 'gallstone' — illustrates what the pilot is reduced to in death: a collection of fragments.
- The irony of 'lucky half crown'.
- 'anchored' suggests something secured very strongly.
- Alliteration in 'steel bars of a stank' suggests something harsh and metallic.
- The Scots dialect word 'stank' helps establish the setting of the poem.
- The humour of 'biting the bullet' and the comparison to someone with a bullet between his teeth. This idiomatic expression also suggests the idea of having to put up with something.
- 'looks like' suggests the ambiguities and uncertainties that pervade the poem.

4.	By referring to this poem and another poem by Don Paterson you have studied discuss how he makes the reader consider the theme of time.	**10**

You can answer this question in bullet points or in a series of linked statements.

Marks are allocated to this question (as they are for all the 10-mark Scottish text questions) as follows:

You will get up to 2 marks for commenting on an area of 'commonality', i.e. pointing out that Nil Nil deals with loss and ultimate extinction over time and that 11:00: Baldovan deals with the frightening and disconcerting changes that the passing of time can bring. A general comment on theme will be worth up to 2 marks.

There are another 2 marks available for referring to the extract – you could refer to:

- 'deeper and deeper obscurity' in the epigraph.
- The gradual extinction through the years of the football club related in the first narrative in the poem.
- The loss of identity suffered by the pilot over time.
- The 'fading', 'failing' and 'thinning down' that takes place as time passes.

Whatever references you choose to make, remember to **comment** *on their effect.*

The remaining 6 marks are allocated for your comments on the other text (11:00: Baldovan) and its presentation of the theme of time. Effective and insightful comments will always score well. Markers will award 3, 2 or 1 marks to each point that you make. For this question you might refer to and comment on:

- The significance of the title.
- The time shift signalled at the end of line 17 'the bus will let us down in another country' and the associated dislocation felt by the speaker.
- The changes to the world described in the poem.
- 'sisters and mothers are fifty years dead'.
- The depiction of the movement from childhood to adulthood.
- The realisation of the destructive power of the passing of time.

© 2015 Leckie & Leckie Ltd

001/30012015

10 9 8 7 6 5

ISBN 9780007554409

Published by
Leckie & Leckie Ltd
An imprint of HarperCollins*Publishers*
Westerhill Road, Bishopbriggs, Glasgow, G64 2QT
T: 0844 576 8126   F: 0844 576 8131
leckieandleckie@harpercollins.co.uk
www.leckieandleckie.co.uk

Publisher: Fiona Burns
Project manager: Craig Balfour

Special thanks to
Jill Laidlaw (copy edit)
Louise Robb (proofread)
Lauren Reid (image research)
QBS (layout)
Ink Tank (cover)

Printed in Italy by Lego S.P.A.

A CIP Catalogue record for this book is available from the British Library.

Acknowledgements
Information on pages 11, 37, 57, 77–81, 94, 96 and 100–101 © Scottish Qualifications Authority; extract from 'Post-traumatic stress disorder is the invisible scar of war' by Stuart Tootal on pages 11–19 © Telegraph Media Group Limited 2014; extract from *The Return of John MacNab* by Andrew Greig on page 24 is reproduced by permission of Quercus Publishing; extracts from *Laidlaw* by William McIlvanney on page 24 are reproduced by permission of Canongate Books; extract from *Romanno Bridge* by Andrew Greig on page 25 is reproduced by permission of Quercus Publishing; extract from 'Pilate's Wife' and 'Mrs Icarus' by Carol Ann Duffy on pages 27 and 28 are reproduced by permission of Pan Macmillan; extract from 'Ambulances' by Philip Larkin on page 30 is reproduced by permission of Faber & Faber; 'Heliographer' by Don Paterson on page 31 is reproduced by permission of Faber & Faber; 'In a snug room' by Norman MacCaig on page 31 is reproduced by permission of Birlinn Ltd.; 'Stopping by Woods on a Snowy Evening' by Robert Frost on page 32 is reproduced by permission of Henry Holt and Company; 'Head of English' by Carol Ann Duffy on page 33 © Carol Ann Duffy and reproduced by permission of the author c/o Rogers, Coleridge & White Ltd.; 'Thrushes' by Ted Hughes on page 34 is reproduced by permission of Faber & Faber; 'Waterfall' by Seamus Heaney on page 34 is reproduced by permission of Faber & Faber; extracts from *All My Sons* by Arthur Miller on page 35 are reproduced by permission of The Wylie Agency (UK) Ltd; extracts from *What Sport Tells Us About Life* by Ed Smith on pages 40–43 are reproduced by permission of Penguin Books Ltd.; extract from 'Youth subcultures: what are they now?' by Alexis Petridis on page 45 is reproduced by permission of Guardian News & Media Ltd; extract from *Crow Country* by Mark Cocker on page 46, published by Vintage and reprinted by permission of The Random House Group Limited.; extract from 'Your child is going to experiment: what teenagers really think' by Suzanne Moore on page 50 is reproduced by permission of Guardian News & Media Ltd; extracts from 'Dangerous Liaisons' by Lucy Mangan on pages 52–53 are reproduced by permission of Guardian News & Media Ltd; extract from 'Stop criticising private schools, start learning from them' on pages 54–55 © Telegraph Media Group Limited 2014; extract from 'Secret Teacher: jargon is ruining our children's education' on pages 55–57 is reproduced by permission of Guardian News & Media Ltd; extract from 'Want to silence a two-year-old? Try teaching it to ride a motorbike' by Charlie Brooker on pages 57–59 is reproduced by permission of Guardian News & Media Ltd; extract from *The Greatest Show on Earth* by Richard Dawkins on pages 61–62, published by Jonathan Cape and reprinted by permission of The Random House Group Limited.; extract from 'Science lessons should tackle creationism and intelligent design' by Professor Michael Reiss on pages 63–64 is reproduced by permission of Guardian News & Media Ltd; extract from 'Visiting Hour' by Norman MacCaig on page 66 is reproduced by permission of Birlinn Ltd.; extract from *The Slab Boys* by John Byrne on pages 68–71 is reproduced by permission of Casarotto Ramsay & Associates Ltd.; extract from *Sunset Song* by Lewis Grassic Gibbon on pages 72–73 is in the public domain; extract from 'Nil Nil' by Don Paterson is reproduced by permission of Faber & Faber

Images
P17 © Jerome Starkey / Contributor / Getty Images; P 20 © Geraint Lewis / Alamy; P31 © © Stephen Finn / Alamy; P35a ID1974 / Shutterstock.com; P35b © Bruce Glikas / Contributor / Getty Images; P36 © John Snelling / Contributor / Getty Images; P38 twiiter logo - © dolphfyn / Shutterstock.com; P40a © snig/ shutterstock.com; P40b © AGIF / Shutterstock.com; P43 © John Cohen / Contributor / Getty Images; P52 © WENN UK / Alamy; P54 © Fred Morley / Stringer / Getty Images; P68 © ZUMA Press, Inc. / Alamy; P75 © Planet News Archive / Contributor / Getty Images; P77 © Igor Bulgarin / Shutterstock.com; P79 © Chris Bull / Alamy; P79 © Geraint Lewis / Alamy; P102 © Chris Jenner / Shutterstock.com; P115 © Maxisport / Shutterstock. com; P115 © s_bukley / Shutterstock.com

All other images © Shutterstock.com